Th

THE CHICAGO HISTORY OF AMERICAN CIVILIZATIO

Daniel J. Boorstin, EDITOR

Confederacy

By Charles P. Roland

THE UNIVERSITY OF CHICAGO PRESS
CHICAGO AND LONDON

To my parents

GRACE AND CLIFFORD ROLAND

THE UNIVERSITY OF CHICAGO PRESS, CHICAGO 60637
The University of Chicago Press, Ltd., London W. C. 1

Editor's Preface

The Southerners who made the Confederacy saw their new nation as a victory over colonialism. They saw themselves in the tradition of anti-imperial wars, of which the American Revolution was the model—wars which have continued into this century. They wished, so they said, to cease being a colony of North and West, and at long last to govern themselves. From their point of view the Civil War was primarily a war for independence and the Confederacy its enduring symbol.

The Confederacy lasted only from February, 1861, until April, 1865. But the Civil War was possible because Southerners long before had begun to think of themselves as a nation. Perhaps the most troubling legacy of the war is that Southerners ever since have found it difficult not to believe that somehow they are a nation within a nation. The drama which Mr. Roland unfolds brilliantly in this volume is only the hectic climax of a much longer story with its last chapter yet to be written.

Mr. Roland shows us the travail, the personal conflict and compromise, of men trying to give political form to an emotional reality. His story reminds us how much we miss if we look upon our nation as the product only of happy coincidences between 1776 and 1789. We can see how much we owe to the wisdom of a Franklin, a Washington, a Jefferson, a Madison, and a John Adams, when we see a Jefferson Davis, a Robert Barnwell Rhett, a William Lowndes Yancey, a Robert Toombs, a Howell Cobb, and an Alexander H. Stephens wrestling with comparable problems. The Federal Constitution appears in a new light after we have seen the South trying to employ it (almost word for word) to build a smaller, decentralized nation. We see the peculiar advantages of our continent-nation when we observe wise and selfless men of one region trying to make a nation out of a piece of our country.

In her brief life the Confederacy accomplished some astonishing feats. In proportion to her population, industrial resources, and wealth, she developed a military power perhaps never equaled in modern times. The Confederacy made one of the greatest communal efforts of all history in the bloodiest war of the nineteenth century. Mr. Roland's story is thus an important early chapter in the history of Americans organized for total war.

The military strength and weakness of the Confederacy, as Mr. Roland is careful to show, was a product of all its institutions. We see, for example, how slavery, which was integral to the Way of Life the South was defending, affected the South's ability to organize defense. We begin to be able to assess the truth of James Madison's prediction, some thirty years earlier, that any country cursed with a servile population cannot win against a people wholly free. Yet Southern leaders saw themselves as defenders and builders. Mr. Roland helps us share the exhilaration and the despair of men committed by their past

Editor's Preface

to create a nation that could not live. Still, many of the problems of the Confederacy have remained the problems of the United States itself.

By relating the story of the Confederacy to all our history, Mr. Roland gives his volume an important place in the "Chicago History of American Civilization," which aims to make each aspect of our culture a window to all our past. The series contains two kinds of books: a *chronological* group, which provides a coherent narrative of American history from its beginning to the present day, and a *topical* group, which deals with the history of varied and significant aspects of American life. This book is one of the topical group.

Daniel J. Boorstin

Table of Contents

Illustrations

MAPS

(Pages xi – xiv)

PLATES

Illustrations

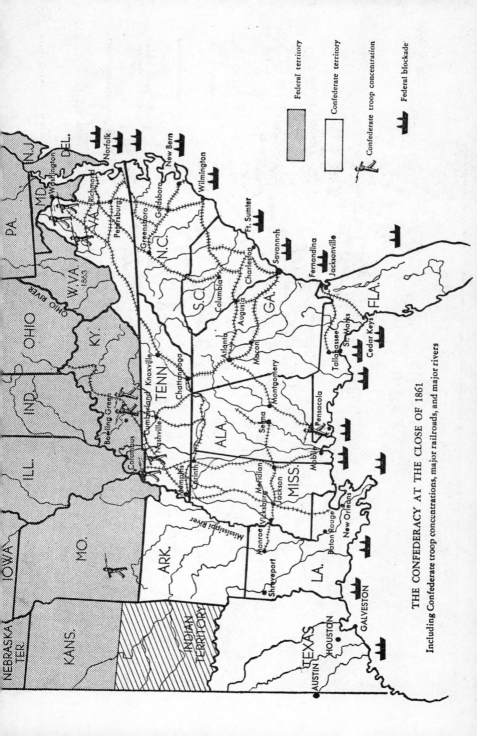

THE CONFEDERACY AT THE CLOSE OF 1861

Including Confederate troop concentrations, major railroads, and major rivers

Federal territory

Confederate territory

Confederate troop concentration

Federal blockade

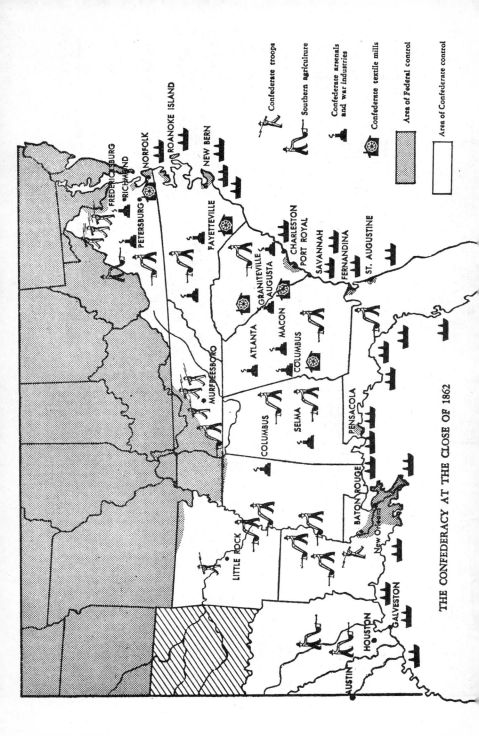

THE CONFEDERACY AT THE CLOSE OF 1862

Confederate troops

Southern agriculture

Confederate arsenals
and war industries

Confederate textile mills

Area of Federal control

Area of Confederate control

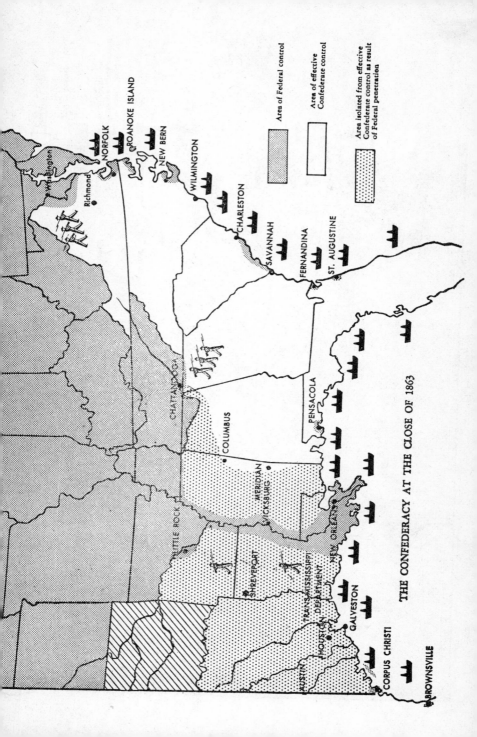

THE CONFEDERACY AT THE CLOSE OF 1863

Area of Federal control

Area of effective
Confederate control

Area isolated from effective
Confederate control as result
of Federal penetration

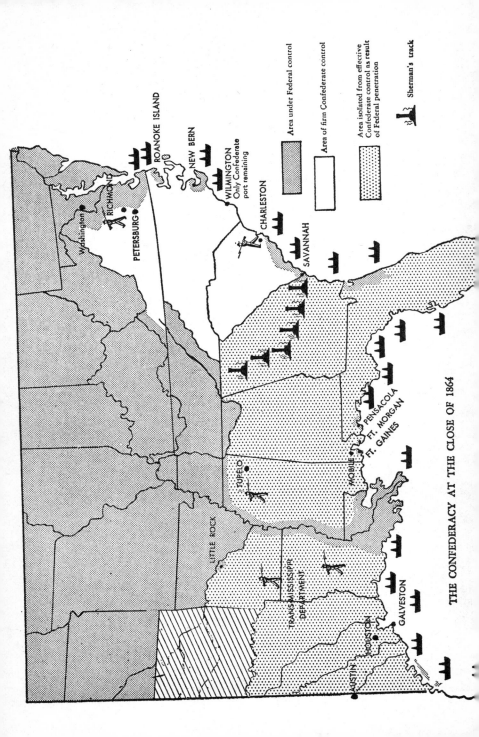

THE CONFEDERACY AT THE CLOSE OF 1864

Area under Federal control

Area of firm Confederate control

Area isolated from effective
Confederate control as result
of Federal penetration

Sherman's track

WASHINGTON
RICHMOND
PETERSBURG
ROANOKE ISLAND
NEW BERN
WILMINGTON
Only Confederate
port remaining
CHARLESTON
SAVANNAH
PENSACOLA
FT. MORGAN
FT. GAINES
MOBILE
TUPELO
LITTLE ROCK
TRANS-MISSISSIPPI
DEPARTMENT
AUSTIN
HOUSTON
GALVESTON

I

The Lower South Departs

A deep silence fell upon the South Carolina Convention as Chancellor John A. Inglis of Chesterfield arose to address the chair. The day was December 20, 1860, a fateful occasion in the history of the American people. Chancellor Inglis solemnly read the Ordinance drafted by his committee:

We the people of the State of South Carolina, in convention assembled, do declare and ordain, and it is hereby declared and ordained, that the Ordinance adopted by us in convention, on the 23rd day of May, in the year of our Lord, seventeen hundred and eighty-eight, whereby the Constitution of the United States was ratified, and also all the acts and part of acts of the General Assembly of this State ratifying amendments of the said Constitution, are hereby repealed, and that the union now subsisting between South Carolina and other States under the name of "United States of America" is hereby dissolved.

Then the Convention cast its votes—"yeas" 169, "nays" none!

News of this momentous decision spread instantly and sent

a mighty wave of exultation across the city of Charleston, where the Convention was being held. An issue of the Charleston *Mercury* appeared miraculously on the streets within five minutes after the vote was taken. Places of business closed. Church bells rang the glad tidings. Artillery thundered from the Citadel. Palmetto flags were everywhere unfurled. Old men burst from their houses and ran shouting down the streets. State military formations paraded in every direction, their music lost in the clamor of a town gone mad with the release of pent-up emotion. An observer later said, "The whole heart of the people had spoken."

The Ordinance was signed that evening with dramatic ceremony in Institute Hall in the presence of the governor and both houses of the legislature. The delegates marched in procession through streets lined with cheering citizens and were greeted as they entered the building by three thousand excited spectators. Hundreds of ladies saluted with handkerchiefs from the galleries. Large palmetto trees stood on either side of the president's chair. For two hours the document passed from delegate to delegate, as outbursts of wild applause greeted the signing of special favorites in the Convention. At last President D. F. Jamison of Barnwell arose and announced, "The Ordinance of Secession has been signed and ratified, and I proclaim the State of South Carolina an independent Commonwealth."

This was the climax of a swift series of events that had begun with the election six weeks earlier of Abraham Lincoln to the presidency of the United States. While the rest of the South waited, the South Carolina legislature, then in session for the task of choosing presidential electors, had begun immediately to discuss the calling of a state convention to decide on the desperate venture of separate state secession. The governors of other Southern states already had indicated their approval of such a course. Mississippi, Alabama, and Florida would follow the lead of another seceding state, said their chief executives. Georgia would not move alone, but would be influenced by the action of other states. North Carolina and Louisiana would not immediately secede, but would oppose the coercion of any states that might choose to do so.

When the South Carolina legislature seemed to hesitate, the people of the state stormily demanded action. The Minute Men of Columbia passed resolutions expressing impatience over the delay and calling for an early convention. A mass meeting of citizens in Charleston was converted into a grand secession rally by the impassioned oratory of visiting speakers from Georgia, who pledged their state to follow the lead of South Carolina. The Charleston *Mercury*, trumpet of secession, upbraided the timidity of the legislators, and private citizens wrote letters scathing the "submissionists." Whatever reservations the lawmakers may have had quickly dissolved in the heat of public demand, and a bill calling for a December convention unanimously passed both houses of the legislature.

The die was cast with this decision. From every portion of the state arose the cry for separation, even from districts that had long been strongholds of Unionism. Young ladies threatened to secede from men who lacked the courage to secede from the old federation. Advocates of secession declared that the people had at last repented of their error and were united against the common foe—the North. On December 6 the voters of the state overwhelmingly elected a convention of secessionist delegates.

The Convention met on December 17 in Columbia, armed

with the encouragement of secessionists from many parts of the lower South. Commissioners from Alabama and Mississippi were there to lend support. Presently Governor M. S. Perry of Florida arrived to bless the proceedings, and prominent citizens from throughout the South came to witness and approve. Stamped upon the minds of the delegates was a recent manifesto by Southern congressmen:

> The argument is exhausted. All hope of relief in the Union . . . is extinguished, and we trust the South will not be deceived by appearances of the pretense of new guarantees. . . . We are satisfied the honor, safety, and independence of the Southern People require the organization of a Southern Confederacy—a result to be obtained only by separate State secession.

The Convention met on the morning of December 17 in the Baptist church in Columbia and elected D. F. Jamison of Barnwell president. Jamison's opening address was a call to action. He declared that the election of secessionist delegates was itself a popular mandate for separation, that constitutional guarantees by the North were no longer to be trusted, and that the highest honor of his life would be to sign an ordinance of secession as chairman of the Convention. He closed with Danton's stirring challenge to the French revolutionists, "To dare! and again to dare! and without end to dare!"

A threatening epidemic of smallpox in Columbia caused the Convention to adjourn to Charleston. But before the move, the intention of the members was made clear in a resolution unanimously passed that the state withdraw from the Union, and that a committee be appointed to draft an ordinance of secession.

Charleston welcomed the delegates with open arms and with the temper of secession clearly written upon her brow. Blue cockades were in every hat. State flags were in full display, and the streets were gay with bunting. On the store fronts hung paintings of wharves piled high with cotton and a harbor bristling with masts—visions of the blessings expected of secession. Crowds of excited citizens lined the streets and packed the squares leading to Institute Hall, where the Convention first met. The word SECESSION was branded in bold black characters upon the gavel that brought the meeting to order. Secession was in the very air, and the Ordinance adopted on December 20 was but the formal statement of a sentiment well-nigh universal in South Carolina.

The secession of South Carolina was the ripened fruit of an ancient political philosophy—the compact theory of government. Planted by European political thinkers of the seventeenth and eighteenth centuries, it had been carefully nurtured by a long line of Southern husbandmen, including Thomas Jefferson, John Taylor of Caroline County, Virginia, Nathaniel Macon of North Carolina, and John Randolph of Roanoke, Virginia. More familiarly known to the people of the South as "state rights," this doctrine received its fullest exposition in the writings of the great South Carolinian John C. Calhoun.

The South Carolina Convention instinctively turned to this philosophy to justify secession and demonstrate its legitimacy. In a Declaration of Immediate Causes, the Convention described the Constitution of the United States as a compact among free, sovereign, and independent states that had originally joined themselves together of their free will and could sever the ties of nationality in the same manner. In a host of ways the states of the North had violated this ancestral compact and rendered it null and void, said the Declaration. They had pronounced slavery a sin, permitted the growth of abolitionist societies, assisted thousands of slaves to escape from their rightful owners, incited servile insurrection, developed a sectional political party inimical to the interests of the entire South, and finally had elevated to the Presidency a man who had openly declared, "This government cannot endure permanently half slave, half free." Once this man was in office, thought the South Carolina seceders, the ancient liberties would be gone, the constitutional guarantees to a minority people cast aside, and self-government dead. The Government of the United States would indeed have become an enemy of the people of the South. In the eyes of the South Carolina Convention, secession was but the formal recognition that the original compact between the state and the Union no longer existed.

Secession was the culmination of a long process in American history. Prophets of rare vision sensed a profound national discord as early as the American Revolution. In 1776 a British observer wrote that American independence would be followed by a bitter contest between North and South because of incompatible economic systems; that the more-numerous Northerners would take control of the government; and that the South would ultimately resort to arms and be conquered. When in 1819 the great controversy arose over the extension of slavery into Missouri and the remainder of the Louisiana Purchase, the aged Thomas Jefferson wrote with foreboding, "This momentous question, like a firebell in the night, awakened and filled me with terror. I consider it at once as the knell of the Union." John Quincy Adams predicted civil war and servile insurrection and admitted in his diary, "So glorious would be its final issue, that, as God shall judge me,

I dare not say that it is not to be desired." The fires of the Missouri controversy were extinguished by political compromise and the public mind temporarily put at ease.

In less than a decade the tariff question arose to vex the American people, for the planters of South Carolina attributed to the protective tariff all of the ills of a depressed agricultural economy. Out of this debate came John C. Calhoun's original exposition of state sovereignty, which served as the justification for the nullification of the tariff act by a South Carolina convention, and ultimately for secession. Again the statesmen of the nation smothered the kindling flame in compromise.

In the 1830's the debate over slavery, quiescent since the Missouri Compromise, burst forth anew as the New England conscience sought to purge the land of this chief among sins. William Lloyd Garrison's *Liberator* denounced the South in the most unrestrained language the nation had ever read, and Southern spokesmen from press, bar, pulpit, and husting answered in kind. Stimulated by the spread of the Cotton Kingdom and stung to fury by the assaults of the abolitionists, the South elevated slavery from the position of a necessary evil to that of a positive good. There was now no possibility of turning back, for a distinct Southern consciousness had been born.

Acquisition of new territory by the United States fanned the flames of sectional controversy. The annexation of Texas and the waging of the Mexican War were denounced in the North as Southern plots to expand the empire of cotton and slavery. When in 1846 Northern congressmen sought by the Wilmot Proviso to prevent the extension of slavery into any land acquired in the war with Mexico, the resentment of the Southern people knew no bounds. Even those who doubted that slavery could thrive in the soil and climate of Mexico damned the proviso as a deliberate insult—a taunting "amen" to the Almighty's decree limiting the cotton area. Certain Southern leaders—among them the fiery Robert Barnwell Rhett of Charleston and William L. Yancey of Alabama—began to urge a resort to the most desperate of remedies, secession. The temper of the nation was ominous.

Indeed, by the mid-1840's the signs of disunion were clear for all with eyes to see. Two of the greatest of the national religious organizations, the Methodist and Baptist churches, then split asunder. Leading theologians of the South were now staunch champions of the "peculiar institution." In 1844 the general conference of the Methodist church asked Bishop James O. Andrew of Georgia to cease his ministry until he had disposed of his Negro slaves. Indignant over this demand, the Southern delegates withdrew and organized the Methodist Episcopal Church, South. Southern Baptists soon took a similar step. John C. Calhoun in 1850 warned Americans that the breaking of these religious cords was a prelude to national division.

The moment of secession seemed to have come when in 1849 California applied for admission to the Union as a free state. Delegates from most of the slave states then met in Nashville, Tennessee, to discuss the course of the South in the crisis. Disunionists, such as Rhett, hoped to persuade the assembly to carry the South out of the Union in a body. The eyes of the Nashville Convention and of the nation turned to Washington, where the greatest political drama of the generation was being enacted in the halls of Congress. This was the passage of the Compromise of 1850, admitting California as a free state, organizing other territories in the Mexican Cession without men-tion of slavery, abolishing the slave trade in the District of Columbia, compensating Texas for land claimed by her that was added to the Territory of New Mexico, and framing a stringent Federal fugitive slave law to placate the South.

The Compromise of 1850 was the final heroic political surgery of the fading Whig statesmen Henry Clay and Daniel Webster, strongly assisted by Democrat Stephen A. Douglas of Illinois. The nation appeared to rally as the people of both North and South hailed the Compromise and congratulated the wisdom of its makers. Apostles of secession watched in disappointment as the Nashville Convention disbanded before a wave of Unionism that swept the South. But the dying Calhoun sensed the impermanency of the Compromise of 1850 and the ultimate defeat of his people, and uttered the anguished cry: "The South! The poor South!"

Calhoun was right. The spirit of compromise vanished as the personal liberty laws of the North made mockery of the fugitive slave act and the expansionists of both sections contended mightily for control of the remaining unsettled portion of the Louisiana Purchase—an area that had been overpassed in the earlier rush of emigrants to Oregon and California. The decade following the Compromise of 1850 was one of mounting tension in which sectional attitudes hardened into dogma and the exhortations of political leaders took on a new belligerency. The North waxed strong in population, industry, and finance; the South turned with renewed devotion to agriculture, repeating the litany coined by David Christy and Senator James H. Hammond of South Carolina, "Cotton is King."

For a generation the Missouri Compromise had stilled the clamor over slavery in the Louisiana Purchase; then in 1854 the Compromise was repealed by the Kansas-Nebraska act, and three years later the Compromise was declared unconstitutional by the Supreme Court in the Dred Scott decision. The entire area of the Louisiana Purchase was now legally open to slavery. In spite of the prevailing thought that slavery had already reached its geographic limits, political leaders of both North and South instantly set up an outcry over the abstract right to extend it. Southern "fire-eaters" (Robert Barnwell Rhett of South Carolina, William L. Yancey of Alabama, and Albert Gallatin Brown of Mississippi) insisted that Congress protect slavery in all of the western territories, while in the North the Republican party came into being, determined that slavery should spread no more. Bloodshed in Kansas between pro-slavery and antislavery settlers clearly portended a greater strife. In 1859, with hands still red from the Kansas massacres, the demented visionary John Brown descended upon the government arsenal at Harper's Ferry, Virginia, resolved to lead the slaves into the promised land of freedom. He was captured and hanged. Ironically, Brown alive failed in his desperate mission; Brown "a-mouldering in the grave" became the sainted martyr of the abolitionist crusade and thus succeeded beyond his maddest dream.

The presidential election of 1860 came upon a nation already divided in spirit. A majority of the Northern people intended to stop the extension of slavery, and the people of the South still burned with anger over John Brown's raid and the eulogies rendered him by Northern spokesmen. The one remaining bond of unity—the Democratic party—now split asunder. Northern Democrats nominated Douglas for President and Hershel V. Johnson of Georgia for Vice President. Their platform advocated leaving to the Supreme Court the question of slavery in the territories; but Douglas had already explained in his famous debates with Abraham Lincoln how slavery could be excluded regardless of what the Court might say. Southern Democrats took the name Constitutional Democratic party and nominated John C. Breckinridge of Kentucky for President and Joseph Lane of Oregon for Vice President. They demanded congressional protection of slavery in the territories. Former members of the defunct Whig party formed the Constitutional Union party and nominated John Bell of Tennessee for President and Edward Everett of Massachusetts for Vice President. Their platform called for supporting the Constitution, the Union, and the laws; these were articles of political faith too exalted to give offense, too passive to win an election.

The Republican party nominated Abraham Lincoln of Illinois and shaped a platform that appealed to every element in the majority North. It advocated that Congress exclude slavery from the territories; it promised free farms to settlers in the national domain in the West; it pledged Federal support to internal improvements, including the building of a railroad to the Pacific; and it called for a protective tariff for the benefit of American industry. This strategy was successful, and Lincoln was victorious. Without any support in the slave states, he won a clear majority of the electoral votes of the nation. The next move was the South's.

The Southern vote in the election of 1860 was not a mandate for secession; if anything, it was the opposite. Three states of the upper South (Kentucky, Tennessee, and Virginia) cast their electoral votes for Bell, thus indicating a preference for Unionism. Breckinridge won the electoral votes of all states in the lower South, plus those of North Carolina and Maryland. But Bell gained a heavy minority popular vote in the lower South, and Unionists Bell and Douglas together received more popular votes in the slave states than did Breckinridge. Moreover, a vote for Breckinridge was not necessarily a vote for disunion, though he probably was supported by all who favored this drastic course. As late as the fall of 1860 a majority of the Southern people were Unionists. But the Unionism of many of them was based upon the expectation that the sectional Republican party would be defeated. Lincoln's election turned the South to secession.

Leading secessionists had since the abortive Nashville Convention of 1850 despaired of achieving "co-operative" secession, that is, the simultaneous secession of the slave states acting through a convention of delegates. This procedure was too unwieldy. Separate state secession held greater promise of success, for it would enable the bolder and more determined states to move immediately; the timid would be inspired to follow.

South Carolina had been carefully groomed by history to lead the procession of withdrawing states. She had produced Calhoun, the high priest of state rights, and she had first put to test his theories in the nullification controversy nearly thirty years earlier. The Nashville Convention had been called at the behest of Carolinians Calhoun and Rhett. Throughout the tense 1850's Rhett's had perhaps been the most insistent voice in the secessionist chorus.

Signs were unmistakable in South Carolina during the presidential election of 1860 that a Republican victory would send the state out of the Union. The few Unionists who dared disagree were branded as Tories and traitors. When the news of Lincoln's election was announced, crowds in Charleston cheered a Southern Confederacy, and the *Mercury* declared that the revolution of 1860 had begun. The issue was never in serious doubt, for the people of the state were almost unanimous in their desire for separation. Within six weeks after Lincoln's election, South Carolina was out of the Union.

What of the other states of the lower South? When South Carolina had nullified the Federal tariff in Jackson's administration she had been alone. No sister state had come to her support. If this should again occur, the plight of the lone commonwealth would be perilous. But the South Carolina Convention in 1860 acted with the assurance that other Southern states would immediately follow the lead of South Carolina and that a Southern Confederacy would soon come into being. This belief was quickly justified by the course of events.

The withdrawal of South Carolina set off the long-threatened chain reaction. Mississippi seceded on January 9, 1861. The issue in this "storm center of secession" was virtually decided from the moment that South Carolina cast her vote; indeed, if some other state had not taken the initiative, Mississippi probably would have done so. On the tenth, Florida declared her independence, and the next day Alabama did the same. The eyes of an anxious nation turned to Georgia, "the empire state of the South."

The decision of Georgia was crucial. Her central location in the deep South made her a vital link between the states of the Atlantic Coast and those of the Gulf; her recently acquired industrial strength was essential to the economy and military stature of a Southern nation; and her statesmen stood high in the councils of the South. The contest was fierce in the Georgia legislature over the question of calling a convention. Former United States Congressman Alexander Stephens, one of the most revered figures in the state, pled that the time had not yet arrived for separation. "This government of our fathers," he affirmed, "with all its defects, comes nearer the objects of all good government than any other on the face of the earth." He was supported by Benjamin H. Hill and Hershel V. Johnson. Other Georgians just as powerful, Senator Robert Toombs, former Secretary of the Treasury Howell Cobb, and his brother T. R. R. Cobb, exhorted the legislature to separate Georgia from the Union without delay. Toombs addressed the lawmakers in flaming phrases, saying: "Throw the bloody spear into this den of incendiaries! . . . Withdraw yourselves from such a Confederacy; it is your right to do so; your duty to do so. . . . Make another war of independence . . . fight its battles over again; reconquer liberty and independence." Later Toombs wired from Washington, "Secession by the 4th of March next should be thundered from the ballot box by the unanimous voice of Georgia." Howell Cobb wrote, "Each hour [after Lincoln's inauguration] that Georgia . . . remains a member of the Union will be an hour of degradation, to be followed by certain and speedy ruin." Georgia followed Toombs and the Cobbs instead of Stephens. On January 19, 1861, after defeating a strong effort to substitute "co-operative" secession for immediate secession, the state convention voted 208 to 89 in favor of separation.

The strength of secessionist conviction in Louisiana was at first doubtful. A flourishing sugar industry was supported by the Federal tariff, and the merchants of New Orleans had strong financial ties with the merchants and bankers of the North. Pockets of Unionism existed among the yeoman farmers of the hill and piney woods parishes in northern Louisiana. In the presidential election a majority of the state's voters had favored Bell or Douglas, though Breckinridge had received a plurality of her popular votes, and hence had won her electoral votes. But in early January a majority of delegates favoring immediate withdrawal from the Union was elected to the state convention on secession. For reasons that can only be surmised, thousands of voters stayed away from the polls in this election. Some historians believe that most of these citizens were opposed to secession, but felt that it was inevitable, and therefore did not take the trouble to vote. Had they done so, they may have held Louisiana in the Union, it is said. Be this as it may, all attempts at "co-operation" in the convention were defeated, and on January 26 the ordinance of secession was passed by a vote of 113 to 17. The Southern nation-in-the-making was assured the port and metropolis of New Orleans.

Texas separatists were faced with the opposition of Governor Sam Houston. But the stern old patriot and nationalist was overridden and finally cast out of office for refusing to take an oath to support the Confederacy. On February 1 a state convention passed an ordinance of secession, and three weeks later this was approved by popular referendum.

All of the states of the lower South were now out of the Union, swept out by a great emotional folk movement. Notwithstanding the presence of large Unionist minorities in some of the states, it is doubtful that any similar political rupture in modern history has been supported by as high a proportion of the population. Historians of today estimate that half of the American Colonists favored severance from England at the outbreak of the American Revolution; John Adams believed that not more than a third of them desired separation. A majority of the people of the lower South approved of secession, for they believed that the North had drifted into dangerous political heresy and that only through independence could the ancestral institutions of the South be preserved.

II

Birth of the Confederacy

For a few weeks the seceded states were in fact independent commonwealths. South Carolinians called their state the "Palmetto Republic." But leaders of the secession movement had in mind from the beginning the formation of a Southern nation embodying their ideals on slavery, economic conservatism, and state rights. On the day that South Carolina withdrew from the Union, Robert Barnwell Rhett introduced a resolution calling for a convention of Southern states for the purpose of forming a national government. Rhett also suggested Montgomery, the capital of Alabama, as a suitable meeting place for such a convention. Possibly at the urging of the South Carolinians, the Alabama secession convention invited the other withdrawing states to send representatives to Montgomery to organize the Confederate States of America.

On February 4, 1861, delegates from six seceded states assembled in the chamber of the Alabama senate in Montgomery to create a Southern republic. They were later joined by the

Texas delegation. The fifty men who made up this group were among the outstanding citizens and political leaders of the South. Seventeen were planters and forty were lawyers, many of whom were state chief and associate justices. A variety of other professions was represented, including physicians, businessmen, teachers, college presidents, editors, and ministers of the Gospel. Almost half of the group had served in the United States Congress. Two had been cabinet members of a President of the United States.

Although some of the leading Southern "fire-eaters" were members of the Convention (including Robert Barnwell Rhett and Louis T. Wigfall of Texas), most of the delegates were conservative in outlook. Many of them were former Whigs and had only recently been converted to secession. Indeed, some of them (especially Alexander Stephens) had never completely surrendered to this persuasion. Nevertheless, the great majority of the group had fully supported the withdrawal of their states and now undertook with singleness of purpose the creation of a new nation.

While the modest little city of Montgomery teemed with anxious and excited visitors from throughout the South, the Convention proceeded swiftly, but with a deep sense of responsibility, to the completion of its task. Howell Cobb of Georgia was elected president of the assembly, and a more distinguished choice could not have been made. Cobb represented the highest in Southern society and statesmanship. Possessing the ample girth of an Elizabethan squire, great personal warmth, and a corresponding breadth of mind and character, he was said to be unquestionably the most popular member of the Convention. An affluent slaveowner, he stood in the top rank of Southern plantation aristocrats. His rich political experience—as former

The Confederacy

Governor of Georgia, Speaker of the United States House of Representatives, and Secretary of the United States Treasury—fitted him admirably for a foremost role in the Southern government. Many friends and supporters hoped to see him at its head. A decade earlier Cobb had been a leading Georgia Unionist, but having despaired of harmony between North and South, he now cast his great influence with the Southern cause and assured the Montgomery assembly that secession was "perfect, complete, and perpetual."

Next came the formation of a provisional government. Need for this was urgent, for it would give immediate unity to the seceded states during the precarious period while a permanent constitution was being written. Christopher Memminger of South Carolina (future Confederate Secretary of the Treasury) was appointed chairman of a committee to draft a Provisional Constitution. The document was quickly prepared and on February 8 unanimously adopted. There was truth in the statement of a participant, "The new provisional government sprang forth as by magic."

The Provisional Constitution was designed to speed the establishment of an interim government and to give direction to the writing of a permanent constitution. The already assembled Convention simply became the Congress of the Provisional Confederate States of North America, with each state having one vote. A Provisional President and Provisional Vice President were to be elected by the Congress, with each state allowed one vote. The Provisional Constitution and Government were supposed to endure for one year from the inauguration of the Provisional President, or until a permanent constitution and government could be put into operation.

Birth of the Confederacy

The most difficult and momentous duty of the Congress was the election of a Provisional President and Vice President. The South possessed many sons who on one count or another could lay legitimate claim to her highest office. Many of these potential candidates were either members of the Montgomery Congress or were present as observers. There were the two great "fire-eaters," Rhett and Yancey, chief contenders for the paternity of the Confederacy; and there were the illustrious Georgians, Cobb, Toombs, and Stephens, all men of outstanding political service in the United States Government. And there was Jefferson Davis of Mississippi, who was not at Montgomery, but whose broad experience in both civil and military administration marked him for an exalted position in the Confederacy.

The men at Montgomery were driven by a great sense of urgency to get the Provisional Government into operation with utmost speed and with a minimum of controversy. This demand for haste and unanimity may explain their choice of Provisional President and Vice President. Customary political maneuvering and posturing were left off, subordinated to the common desire to create a new government without delay. This seems to have been an election largely without "electioneering," management, bargaining, or commitments.

But the desire for speed did not altogether eliminate the differences of opinion as to who the high officials should be. After the adoption of the Provisional Constitution a motion was made to hold the Congress in session and elect immediately the Provisional President and Vice President. The motion was defeated, for many of the delegates wished to hold state caucuses to discuss this important issue. The final selection of candidates was made between the adjournment of the Congress at midnight of February 8 and the time it reconvened at noon of the ninth.

The Southern "extremists" Rhett and Yancey received no serious consideration. Rhett lacked even the support of his fellow South Carolinians, who, though they felt him a man of great devotion to the cause of the South, yet considered him too impulsive and indiscreet for true statesmanship. Yancey was said to have bowed out of the picture in order to make secession more palatable to the Virginians, who, ironically, feared that his militancy would surely bring conflict with the North. Thus, like Sam Adams and Patrick Henry of the American Revolution, the most influential leaders of the Southern revolution were passed over in favor of men of moderation. The three names most frequently on the tongues of the Montgomery delegates were Toombs, Cobb, and Davis.

Many Southerners favored Toombs or Cobb for the highest Confederate position. Toombs was a man of Falstaffian proportions and temperament. Son of an affluent cotton planter, Toombs had risen swiftly on the wings of his powerful oratory, contagious good humor, and unerring political intuition to the highest level in the Whig party in his state. In 1844, while yet in his mid-thirties, he was elected to the United States Congress, and soon he moved into the Senate. Motivated throughout most of his political life by a strong love of the Union, Toombs in 1850 threw his great influence against the forces of separatism in Georgia. Converted to the Democratic party by the great divisive episodes of the 1850's, Toombs became one of the most militant of secessionists. He now appeared to many as the likeliest man to lead the South to independence.

President
Jefferson Davis.
Photograph by
Mathew Brady

Vice President
Alexander Stephens.
Photograph by
Mathew Brady
(Culver Service)

President and Mrs. Jefferson Davis at a reception. Pen drawing
by William Ludwell Sheppard (1833–1912)
(Valentine Museum)

Birth of the Confederacy

Possibly an embarrassment of riches in the Georgia delegation prevented the selection of either Toombs or Cobb for the highest Confederate office. The preference of the Georgians was split, with a slight majority (including his brother) favoring Cobb. The South Carolinians were undecided as between Cobb and Davis. Failure of either of these influential state groups to give undivided support to a candidate afforded opportunity to the Mississippi, Alabama, and Florida delegations to advance their advocacy of Davis. Seeing the Georgia delegation unable to agree on one of their own, the South Carolinians turned to Davis, and finally the representatives of Louisiana and Georgia fell in line for the Mississippian.

The method of selecting a Confederate Vice Presidential nominee appears to have been as paradoxical then as it usually is with political parties today. Alexander Stephens was ruled out as a choice for the presidency because of his opposition to the secession of Georgia, an action that made many Southerners accurately sense that his heart was not fully with the cause of independence. But when the Georgia delegation withdrew the names of Cobb and Toombs in shifting their support to Davis, they submitted the name of Stephens for the second Confederate office, and the other states accepted him in order to give the "empire state" a consolation offering.

On February 9 Davis and Stephens were elected as the Congress had wished it—unanimously and on the first ballot.

President Davis was the incarnation of the virtues and weaknesses of the South. Born in Kentucky in 1808 of yeoman stock, he was educated at Transylvania University and the United States Military Academy in the classical and martial traditions dear to the heart of the South. In 1835 Davis resigned his commission in the United States Army in order to marry the girl he loved, for her father (Colonel Zachary Taylor, future President of the United States) disapproved of the union. Davis' bride died three months after the wedding, but he settled in Mississippi, where, with the aid of a wealthy elder brother, he became a successful cotton planter. Ten years after the death of his first wife, Davis was married to spirited Varina Howell of Natchez. His leisure was devoted to reading in preparation for political leadership, and in 1845 he was elected as a Democrat to the United States House of Representatives. Commanding a Mississippi volunteer regiment during the Mexican War, Davis became the state's most celebrated soldier. In 1847 he was sent to the United States Senate, where he became one of the foremost leaders of the proslavery cause. Defeated in 1851 in running for the governorship of Mississippi on a platform of opposition to the Compromise of 1850, Davis soon escaped from political eclipse by being appointed Secretary of War by President Franklin Pierce. As a distinguished cabinet member, and again later in the United States Senate, Davis was the champion of Southern interests, foreign and domestic. But he was no longer a Southern "extremist"; he had become a Southern "moderate."

Davis was tall, slender, and striking, with features too sharp to be handsome. He was a man of indomitable will, strong intellect, and unquestioned physical and moral courage. Though he exhibited great warmth toward close friends and the members of his family, he possessed the traditional Southern aristocratic sensitivity on matters of personal honor or his prerogatives as a public official. He was capable of sublime self-sacrifice in the interest of the South and at the same time of carping pettiness in dealing with subordinates and critics. Too strong to understand the weak, he was yet too narrow of vision to appreciate the strength of many who shared his cause.

Vice President Alexander Stephens epitomized the fatal rift in the psyche of the South. Stephens served the state of Georgia with distinction in the United States Congress from 1843 until 1859, when he retired to follow a private law practice. Beginning his political career as a Whig, Stephens crossed into the Democratic party under the stress of sectional controversy during the 1850's. His keen and comprehensive mind was housed in a diminutive, sickly body that was to him a life-long source of embarrassment, pain, and despair. Known throughout Georgia as "Little Ellick," he was a gifted political leader and one of the state's most highly respected men. Both before and after becoming Vice President of the Confederacy, Stephens possessed a great affection for the Union and the Federal Constitution. Though his interpretation of the Constitution upheld the principle of state rights—even of secession—he supported Douglas in the presidential campaign of 1860 and opposed the withdrawal of Georgia from the Union. The fullest application of state rights Stephens ultimately would turn against the creature of state rights—the Confederacy.

The emissaries sent by the Montgomery Congress to notify Jefferson Davis of his election found him in the rose garden of his plantation. He had not solicited, nor did he desire, the position of President of the Confederacy. Mississippi had upon her withdrawal from the Union made him commander in chief of the state military forces, and his preference was for a martial career. But when the presidency was offered to him, he accepted it as a solemn duty as well as a high honor.

Davis left immediately for Montgomery. His journey to the

provisional Confederate capital was a wide sweep by rail that took him as far north and east as Chattanooga and Atlanta, and it called forth a great popular ovation as thousands of enthusiastic Southerners greeted him along the way. He arrived at his destination on February 15, to be welcomed by additional throngs of admirers and by the silvery tongued Yancey, who declared, "The man and the hour have met."

At one o'clock on the afternoon of February 18, Davis stood between the tall Grecian columns on the portico of the Alabama state house and was inaugurated Provisional President of the Confederacy. The day was fair and the occasion auspicious. A hushed multitude from the four corners of the South heard the dignified Mississippian affirm the strength, righteousness, and peaceful intention of the Southern republic. The Confederacy was a living example, he said, of the great American principle that governments rest upon the consent of the governed, and that it is the right of the people to alter or abolish those governments whenever they become destructive of the ends for which they were established. The Union from which the Southern states were withdrawn had been perverted from the course of just government, he declared, and the verdict of God and history would uphold the people of the South in their decision. A mutual interest ought to promote peace and commerce between the Northern and Southern nations, he asserted, "But, if this be denied to us, and the integrity of our territory and jurisdiction be assailed, it will but remain for us, with firm resolve, to appeal to arms and invoke the blessings of Providence on a just cause." The address ended to a roar of applause and a salute of artillery, and a band struck up a stirring air called "Dixie." That night the President held a grand reception, and the city was filled with merriment. This was the Confederacy's gladdest hour.

The Montgomery Congress moved immediately after the election of a President and Vice President to the creation of a permanent constitution. With Rhett as chairman, a committee composed of two members from each state drafted the document, and on March 11 the Constitution of the Confederate States of America was unanimously adopted.

In many ways the Confederate organic law followed closely that of the United States. This was to be expected, for the "old Constitution" was universally revered in the South, and the Confederate instrument of government was considered largely a return to its original principles. Alexander Stephens was especially insistent on this point and consented to serve in the Montgomery Convention only after being assured by the Georgia delegation that every effort would be made to write a new constitution as nearly as possible like the old.

The Confederate Constitution provided for a government of three distinct branches: executive, legislative, and judicial. Executive power was vested in a President to be elected by the people of the states through an electoral college. President and Vice President were to serve for a term of six years, and the President was not again eligible for the office. Legislative power resided in a Congress of two houses, with a Senate to be composed of two members from each state and a House of Representatives in which the states were represented on the basis of population. All free persons, excluding Indians not taxed, and three-fifths of the Negro slaves were to be counted for this apportionment. Judicial authority rested in a Supreme Court whose members were to be appointed by the President, with the advice and consent of the Senate, and in such inferior courts as Congress might see fit to create. The principles of the American Bill of Rights were embodied in the Confederate fundamental law.

Features of the Confederate Constitution that differed most significantly from the United States Constitution were those designed to sustain the conservative, agrarian, slave-supported society and economy of the South. In order to forestall in the Confederacy such a debate as had raged in the Union over the question of whether the Constitution were the creature of the people or of the states, the Confederate instrument declared itself to be the work of ". . . the people of the Confederate States, each State acting in its sovereign and independent character." Slavery was called by name instead of by the euphemisms employed in the Federal organ. No law could be passed by the Confederacy denying or impairing the right to own slaves, and the Confederate Congress was to protect the institution of slavery in territories belonging to or acquired by the Confederacy. Importation of slaves was forbidden, except from the United States; Congress was empowered to halt altogether the introduction of slaves. Bounties, protective tariffs for the fostering of industry, and general appropriations for internal improvements were prohibited. Duties could be placed on imports for revenue only. On the other hand, the Constitution opened to the Confederacy a source of income that was denied under the Federal organic law; by two-thirds majority in both houses, Congress could tax exports and thus draw financial support from commerce in the South's great agricultural staples. The President was authorized to veto separate items of appropriations bills, and Confederate cabinet members were permitted, upon approval of Congress, to sit in the legislative body for the discussion of measures pertinent to their departments. The famous "elastic clause," or general welfare provision, of the Federal Constitution was omitted, for Southern statesmen looked upon it as one of the main channels through which the North had drifted into political apostasy.

The Confederate instrument of government was strangely silent on the right of secession or nullification. Instead, it declared the Constitution, laws, and treaties of the Confederacy to be the supreme law of the land. This omission represented more than simply the presumption of the right of secession; Rhett pressed for a positive declaration supporting it and was overruled. Possibly a majority of the delegates sensed the eternal paradox of a government founded by revolution; that an acknowledgment of the right of revolution in its subordinate parts can lead to its own dismembering. Although Davis said that the Confederate Constitution did not admit of a "coerced association of states," the spirit of Southern nationalism ran too strong in the Montgomery Convention to permit an explicit affirmation of the very principle upon which the Confederacy was founded.

Even as the permanent Constitution was being fashioned, the Provisional Government of the Confederacy proceeded with affairs of state. While the Montgomery assembly acted as a Congress by day and a Constitutional Convention by night, Davis selected his cabinet and went about the establishment of a stable administration. Appointments were made according to the ability of the men and with an effort to give representation to as many states as possible. Toombs was named Secretary of State; Christopher G. Memminger of South Carolina, Secretary of the Treasury; Leroy P. Walker of Alabama, Secretary of War; Stephen R. Mallory of Florida, Secretary of the Navy;

The Confederacy

Judah P. Benjamin of Louisiana, Attorney General; and John H. Reagan of Texas, Postmaster General. These selections were greeted with general approval throughout the South; the right men were said to be in the right places.

Davis and his cabinet faced a bewildering array of problems. A workable government had to be formed upon the principles laid down in the Constitution; an army and navy must be created; and a monetary and revenue system established. The Montgomery Congress wisely retained the main fabric of the Federal law in order to ease the transition from Union to Confederacy. All United States statutes as of November, 1860, that were compatible with the Confederate Constitution and not specifically repealed by the Confederate Congress were declared still in effect. Meantime, a committee was selected to revise all statutes and bring them into accord with the new Constitution. Federal employees in the postal and customs services in the South were continued in office, thereby maintaining a core of trained civil servants. The Confederacy salvaged and absorbed into itself as much as possible of the law and administration of the parent government.

The most delicate issue before Davis and his cabinet was that of relations with the United States. The Southern President sincerely wished for harmony with the North, though he feared that this would be impossible. One of his first acts was to commission three agents (André Roman of Louisiana, Martin J. Crawford of Georgia, and John Forsyth of Alabama) to represent the Confederacy in Washington.

The point of severest friction between the two governments was the continued occupation by Federal troops of certain United States forts within the seceded states. Southern leaders insisted that this property now belonged to the withdrawing states or to the new nation created by them. Most of the forts were, upon demand, turned over to local authorities. But the commanding officers of Fort Sumter in Charleston harbor, Fort Taylor at Key West, and Forts Pickens and Jefferson at Pensacola refused to give up these positions. Smarting at this affront to their sovereignty, the South Carolinians prepared to take Fort Sumter by force, and demanded that the Confederacy do so if it could not be acquired through diplomacy. President James Buchanan was torn between disbelief in the right of secession and an equally sincere abhorrence of Federal coercion. He would not surrender the forts, yet he took no punitive action when in January, 1861, a ship bearing provisions for the ill-supplied garrison of Fort Sumter was fired upon and driven away by South Carolina batteries. This was the dangerous impasse inherited by Jefferson Davis and Abraham Lincoln as they entered upon their duties.

The Lincoln cabinet was split on the issue, with Secretary of State William H. Seward (and apparently initially the President also) in favor of the evacuation of Fort Sumter. Seward unofficially assured the Confederate commissioners that this would be done. But Lincoln kept his own counsel and in early April dispatched a fleet with provisions for the Charleston garrison. The Davis administration faced the bitter decision of whether to submit to a permanent Federal occupation of territory within the Confederacy or seize the fort and run the hazard of war.

Pressure upon Davis to seize the fort was fierce. Two months earlier the Provisional Congress had resolved that this ought to be done and had authorized the President to take necessary steps for its accomplishment. The people of South Carolina urged that an attack upon Fort Sumter was long overdue; they

The Confederacy

had been on the point of independent action when in March the Confederate Government had assumed control and ordered General P. G. T. Beauregard to the command. On April 9, after receiving word of Lincoln's relief expedition, Davis assembled his cabinet for the momentous decision. Although the gravity of the situation was obvious, the entire group favored stern measures, with the possible exception of Toombs. According to one source that pictures the aggressive Georgian in an unaccustomed mood of caution, Toombs opposed any drastic move and cried: "It is suicide, it is murder, and will lose us every friend at the North. You will wantonly strike a hornets' nest which extends from mountains to ocean; and legions, now quiet, will swarm out to sting us to death. . . . It is unnecessary, it puts us in the wrong. It is fatal." If the Secretary of State made such remonstrance, he was overruled; Secretary of War Walker instructed Beauregard to demand evacuation of the fort and, if refused, to reduce it.

From noon until after midnight of April 11, Beauregard attempted to induce Major Robert J. Anderson, commander at Fort Sumter, to give up the position without compelling a resort to force. Anderson's final reply was considered unsatisfactory, and before dawn of the twelfth the bombardment began. It lasted through that day and most of the next, and on the thirteenth Anderson surrendered. The people of Charleston looked on from their rooftops and were overwhelmed with emotion. Governor Francis W. Pickens of South Carolina solemnly declared, "Thank God the war is open . . . we will conquer or perish."

Pickens was right. The attack upon Fort Sumter galvanized Lincoln into action, and on April 15 he issued his call to the various state governors for 75,000 troops to be used in maintaining Federal authority in the seceded states. Historians have long disputed over Lincoln's behavior in the course of events that led to Fort Sumter. Some say that he played a Machiavellian game with the Southern leaders, cunningly provoking them into firing the first shot, and thus consolidated his crumbling administration and the masses of the Northern people behind a great patriotic effort to preserve the Union. Lincoln's defenders say no, that he wrestled strenuously with a supremely perplexing issue and was finally unable to avert war and at the same time discharge his duty as President of the United States. However this may be, the actual effects of Fort Sumter seem beyond controversy; the Northern people rose up in a mighty wrath to chastise those who dared lay violent hands upon the flag. The sin of rebellion must be expiated in fire.

Lincoln's call for troops turned the states of the upper South to secession. Citizens of Virginia, North Carolina, Tennessee, and Arkansas had looked with troubled eyes upon the events leading to Fort Sumter, cruelly torn between contending loyalties. They were Southerners by blood and tradition, owning slaves and plantations, and believing theoretically in the right of secession. Yet the spirit of American nationalism burned high in them; the Virginians felt that their forefathers had sired the Union, and the Tennesseans gloried in the belief that their greatest hero, Andrew Jackson, had been its staunchest defender against foes foreign and domestic. The opposing choices of secession or Federal coercion presented an inescapable dilemma; to recoil from one extremity was to be ensnared in the other.

All of these states initially considered and rejected secession. Virginia, along with Kentucky, took the lead in attempting through the art of political compromise to maintain peace in the nation. The Virginia legislature in February called a national convention that met in Washington with ex-President John Tyler in the chair to try to discover the means of reconciliation. Proposals of the convention were similar to those of the famous Crittenden Compromise; they called for the extension of the Missouri Compromise line through the remainder of the western territories, separating free soil from slave soil along the 36° 30′ parallel of latitude, and for the adoption of irrepealable constitutional guarantees of slavery where it already existed. Lincoln was willing to support a constitutional amendment guaranteeing slavery in the states, but he insisted upon the principles of the Wilmot Proviso: slavery must spread no more in the western territories. This half-a-loaf was unacceptable to the leaders of the lower South, and all efforts at compromise failed. Yet the people of the upper South waited and hoped to escape the bitter cup of secession.

Lincoln now demanded the impossible: that they wage war upon their own kind. His call for troops was scornfully rejected by the governors of all the states of the upper South. Even Unionist Governor John Letcher of Virginia spurned the requisition with the declaration that Lincoln had inaugurated civil war. On April 17 a Virginia convention adopted an ordinance of secession, and one month later it was ratified by popular referendum. In the meantime, the state joined the Confederacy. Conventions in Arkansas and North Carolina voted these states out of the Union on May 6 and 20. The Tennessee legislature declared the state to be independent and joined the Confederacy, and on June 8 these measures were approved by popular vote.

By summer 1861 secession had run its course. Eleven states spreading from the Potomac to the Rio Grande were out of the Union and in the Confederacy. Four other slave states—Kentucky, Missouri, Maryland, and Delaware—were destined not to secede, though sympathy for the South was strong in all of them. Confederate "governments in exile" were established for Kentucky and Missouri, and the Confederate flag bore stars representing these two states. Many of the leaders of the South had at first predicted a peaceful dissolution of the Union; some had gone so far as to promise to wipe up with their handkerchiefs all of the blood shed as the result of secession. This illusion was now gone, dispelled by the guns at Fort Sumter and Lincoln's call to action. The forces were gathering for the great strife that was about to burst upon the land.

III

The South Prepares for War

President Jefferson Davis told the world in his inaugural address in Montgomery that if assailed the Confederacy would resort to arms and invoke the blessings of Providence upon her cause. This stern promise was faithfully kept, and for four bitter years the leaders of the South strove mightily to forge a lasting Republic in the flames of war. In the end they failed, for the task was formidable and the odds against them exceedingly great.

The two antagonists were vastly unequal in the resources of war. The most obvious disparity in strength was that of population. The eleven seceded states contained a total population of about 9,000,000 as opposed to 22,000,000 inhabitants in the North. In the population of the South were 3,500,000 Negro slaves, who as laborers would play an important role in helping to sustain the Southern economy and war effort, but would not be used as soldiers by the Confederate government.

Thus the Confederacy denied herself the military services of more than one-third of her entire strength in men.

The Northern advantage in manpower was greatly enhanced from other sources as the war progressed. Hundreds of thousands of Europeans swelled the Federal armies, drawn to the United States by the lure of financial bounties and free land; and ultimately more than 100,000 ex-slaves from areas of the South penetrated by the Northern forces were enlisted into the ranks of their liberators. Additional thousands of men from Unionist portions of the South—especially from the mountainous, non-slave-holding areas of western Virginia and North Carolina and eastern Tennessee—increased the Northern forces. This loss to the Confederacy was offset, however, by Southern sympathy in a number of Union states and by the remoteness of the Pacific Coast, which provided relatively few soldiers to the North.

Even more significant than Northern superiority in manpower was her advantage in industrial resources. For the Civil War was the precursor of the great modern wars; it was a contest of industry against industry and economy against economy, as well as of men against men. The South was woefully unsuited to such a conflict. In 1860 she manufactured less than one-tenth of the industrial goods produced in the United States. Nor does this ratio indicate the true disparity in strength between the two antagonists, since much of the industry of the South was subsidiary to her agricultural economy, devoted to crude and unfinished wares, farm machinery, and household implements—materials not readily convertible to military use. At the outbreak of war the North produced annually, according to value, 17 times as much cotton and woolen goods as did the South; 30 times as many boots and shoes; 20 times as much pig iron; 13 times as much bar, sheet, and railroad iron; 24 times as many locomotive engines; more than 500 times as much general hardware; 17 times as much agricultural machinery; 32 times as many firearms; and 11 times as many ships and boats. Furthermore, the South was completely lacking in other branches of manufacture essential to an independent industrial system. She manufactured no steel, no car wheels, and no sewing machines. Of especial significance to a nation about to enter a mortal trial of arms, she had no munitions industry. Perhaps most damaging of all, the South possessed none of the "parent industries"—none of the machine tools that produce the machinery to turn out the implements of war. In 1865 the United States census taker said, "It was mainly for the want of these [resources], and not for lack of courage, will, or skill, that the revolt failed."

Leaders of the Confederacy depended upon agriculture as the major source of Southern strength, in war as in peace. But Southern agriculture was ill-suited to the support of a prolonged conflict. The region's peacetime economy was based chiefly on the export of cotton to the mills of England and New England, and thus was highly vulnerable to naval blockade. Even without blockade, the Confederacy would be forced by extended hostilities with the North to divert much of her soil to the production of food for the sustenance of armies and civilian population. Lacking a strong domestic industry, she would then be deprived of the immense sums of money required for the sinews of war. In view of the sublime faith of the Southern people in their agrarian way of life, it is one of the ironies of the Civil War that Northern agriculture proved to be as strong a military asset as did Southern agriculture. The farms of the North in 1860 exceeded in value those of the

South; and the output of Northern farms when combined with Northern industrial production created a balanced and self-sufficient economy ideal for the support of war. The South found in the plow and reaper antagonists as formidable as the forge and lathe.

The Confederacy faced still other disadvantages. She possessed less than half as much railway mileage as the North had and few of the facilities for repairing and maintaining her tracks and rolling stock. She had no naval vessels, relatively few merchantmen, and virtually no yards in which to construct ships of either kind. Whereas the Union possessed a regular army and navy—albeit the first of these was severely maimed by secession and the ensuing resignation of Southern officers—the Confederacy had to begin with nothing in the creation of both. Unlike most nations of the world, the South was protected by no formidable geographic barriers; her major terrain features were in most instances aids rather than hindrances to hostile invasion. The Southern mountains ran north and south through the middle of the region, thus isolating the sections of the Confederacy from one another instead of shutting her off from the foe. The great western rivers—the Mississippi, Tennessee, and Cumberland—appeared to have been traced in the earth by some giant strategist planning an invasion of the South; from a point of convergence within Federal territory, they spread like the ribs of a fan into the vitals of the Confederacy. Unable to control the bordering seas, the South was obliged to wage war with flank and rear continuously exposed to invasion.

The Confederacy was beset with liabilities less tangible but no less real than her want of material resources and natural frontiers. Secession was undertaken at a moment in world history singularly inauspicious to its success. In an epoch that saw the final consolidation of many leading nations of Europe, the Southern effort to gain independence was regarded as an unpardonable sin against the prevailing religion of nationalism. This not only served to kindle in Northern hearts an implacable determination to suppress the rebellion, but it left sparks of doubt in the minds of many Southerners. Aside from the celebrated loyalty to the United States of the mountain people of Virginia, North Carolina, and Tennessee, innumerable smaller islands of Unionism remained scattered throughout the South. In curious juxtaposition to this lingering spirit of American nationalism was the opposing principle of state rights; both would be quickened by adversity into sources of defeat for the Confederacy.

The final weakness of the South was the institution of slavery. Not only did it deprive the Confederacy of large numbers of soldiers; in an era of rising belief in the rationality of man and the imminence of an earthly Utopia, it placed the Southern republic under the stigma of fighting to perpetuate an irrational and immoral social order. Leaders of the North were able to convert a war initially undertaken to preserve the Union into a mighty crusade to strike the chains from the arms of millions of men.

The many serious weaknesses of the South were partially offset by certain advantages rising out of her own nature and the nature of the conflict that she waged. She was engaged in a defensive war, which for strategic reasons traditionally requires fewer troops and physical resources than an offensive effort. Her leaders were able to invoke a heroic defense of hearth and home, and thus appeal to the patriotism of all Southerners regardless of their views on slavery or secession. The

South was rich in military leadership, for the profession of arms was highly regarded among her aristocratic plantation society. The Confederate army contained more than three hundred graduates of West Point, including many who were considered the finest of the lot. It has been said that no people ever committed themselves to mortal combat under officers more brilliant than those of the South. Nearly one hundred years after the Civil War a student of history and connoisseur of military leadership, Winston Churchill, would write of the Confederacy's most famous soldier, "[Robert E. Lee] was one of the noblest Americans who ever lived, and one of the greatest captains known to the annals of war." Other Southern officers who either possessed or would achieve distinction were Albert Sidney and Joseph E. Johnston, P. G. T. Beauregard and Thomas J. "Stonewall" Jackson.

The general military policy of President Davis and his counselors was that of defense. This carried into the field of strategy the prevailing Southern idea that secession and the formation of the Confederacy were peaceful acts and ought to be so regarded by the Federal government. Only if attacked would the South fight, and then for the sole purpose of repelling invasion. Impulsive Southerners like Toombs and Governor Henry A. Wise of Virginia were unheeded in their urging of a strategy of aggressiveness. Certain Confederate generals, including Jackson, Beauregard, and Joseph E. Johnston, also at one time or another advocated the offensive. They called for a lightning stroke against the people of the North, before her superior resources could be mobilized. Many scholars have indorsed this as the only hope for Southern victory, pointing out that in a prolonged war of attrition the Confederacy was foredoomed to defeat. Historian E. Merton Coulter concludes that the defensive policy was "disastrous and soul-killing" to the South.

Yet the case for the defensive has merit. Southern leaders felt that an assault upon the North would consolidate every element of her population behind a mighty defense of their homeland; in other words, it would give away to the enemy one of the chief advantages of the Confederacy. Many Southerners who would fight to expel invaders would not support an attack upon the North. Such a move would also tend to alienate foreign sympathy for the South, which from the beginning the Davis administration hoped to cultivate. Finally, the inferior resources of the South would seem to have rendered impossible a successful war of aggression against the North. Four years of prodigious fighting were required in the conquest of the Confederacy by the vastly more powerful Union; that the weaker South could have conquered the North is unthinkable. The argument for a Confederate policy of aggressiveness assumes that the South with her smaller armies could have won on enemy soil victories comparable to or more striking than those she gained at home and that the Northern people would have been so demoralized by initial defeat that they would have given up the struggle. Or that England and France would have been induced by early Confederate successes in the North to intervene in behalf of the South. All of these assumptions are highly problematical. Moreover, Davis and his associates could not know what the historians now know: that the defensive was tried by the Confederacy and found wanting. Southern strategists were aware that defensive wars of separation had often been successful. They knew that the United States had gained her freedom through defensive warfare, and they looked upon the American Revolution as the great prototype of their own war for independence. Professor Clement Eaton is probably right in saying that the defensive policy of the Confederacy was "basically sound."

Morale of the Southern people was at high flame and their confidence in President Davis unbounded during the early days of the Confederacy. The famous English newspaper correspondent, William Howard Russell, found their faith in the cause of independence to be "indomitable." He was repeatedly asked, "Have you seen our President, sir? Don't you think him a very able man?" Russell was of the opinion that such unanimity regarding the character of the Chief Executive would be a source of immense strength in the impending conflict. Spokesmen of the region felt that with trusted slaves to grow the necessary food and cotton, and with Southern youth to perform prodigies of valor on the battlefield, the Confederacy would be invincible. Questions concerning the sources of economic strength for the waging of a mighty war were blithely waved aside. "With France and England to pour gold into their lap with which to purchase all they need in the contest," said Russell, "they believe they can beat all the powers of the Northern world in arms." Exuberant Southerners cried, "Cotton is King," and prophesied that without the white fiber the industries of Europe and of the North would soon be prostrate.

The burning enthusiasm for the cause of an infant republic was contagious, and many who had initially bridled at secession now closed ranks in an effort to make the Confederacy a lasting reality. The Davis administration seemed to be succeeding in the hazardous experiment of creating an authentic nation in the fires of revolution. As in the movement for American independence from Great Britain, this must be accomplished if the South were to be free. For the people of the region were not sharply distinguished from the parent society by history, government, religion, language, or cultural or ethnic characteristics. A sense of Southern nationalism was therefore not complete and pervasive; it must be fully developed in the war itself, if at all. Davis recognized this principle when he said: "The recollections of this great contest, with all its common traditions of glory, of sacrifice and blood, will be the bond of harmony and enduring affection amongst the people, producing unity in policy, fraternity in sentiment, and just effort in war." He could rightly feel at the end of his first year of leadership that he had nurtured these binding emotions.

Major features of Confederate policy were fashioned by the Davis administration at the beginning of Southern independence, while the Mississippian was yet Provisional President and the tide of popular confidence still ran strong. The core of his policy was Southern nationalism. Scholars have explained this as being the result of history; Davis was a product of the new, virile, expansive Southwest where the spirit of sectional solidarity—crystallized by secession into Southern nationalism—was much stronger than that of state rights. Davis had a strong attachment for the state-rights doctrines of Calhoun and had freely employed them in shaping a political strategy for the South as long as she was a minority within the Union, but he was enough of a practical statesman to know that strength lay in unity of purpose and action. State rights in practice was the antithesis of unity, and therefore of strength. This unity, Davis idealistically believed, was to be achieved, not through coercion, but through "homogeneity of interest, policy, and feeling." At least until the South was free, she must be a consolidated nation, and not an aggregate of sovereign states.

The South Prepares for War

The fullest embodiment of this nationalism lay in the Confederate army, whose very existence was a departure from state rights in the strictest sense. Even before the initial inauguration of Davis, and before the coming of war, the Provisional Congress had begun the fashioning of a national army and the construction of an armory and gunpowder factory. The Chief Executive was in full accord with this program and soon strengthened its nationalistic character by causing all military contracts to be approved by the Confederate Secretary of War. To this position, Davis appointed Leroy Pope Walker, a lean Alabama lawyer and "fire-eater."

Walker ultimately proved unequal to the task of directing the military establishment of the Southern republic in a conflict as great as the Civil War. But Walker was a man of some drive and imagination, and he was a Southern nationalist. Under his direction the army began to take shape in the spring of 1861. States were called upon to raise and equip assigned quotas of troops and send them to various points for service in the army of the Confederacy, and volunteers were accepted individually. Purchasing agents were commissioned to procure arms and supplies in the South, in the North, and in Europe. The administration pressed for an act of Congress requiring that enlistments into the army could be made only for the duration of the war. Unable to persuade the lawmakers to lengthen the term of service beyond twelve months, Walker accepted men for this period, provided they came fully armed by their states. Those who came without weapons and were to be equipped by the Confederate government were obliged to volunteer for the duration of the struggle.

Shortage of arms and equipment was initially more acute than want of men. For in the early flush of independence, before defeat and want had dulled their enthusiasm, the men of the South swarmed in great numbers to the Confederacy's colors; in July, 1861, Walker declared that 200,000 additional volunteers could be enlisted within two months if only they could be armed. But the new nation lacked facilities to supply so great a demand on such brief notice, and the government armories were still being built. Thousands of eager men had to be turned away from the enlistment offices.

Nevertheless, the Davis administration and the people of the South wrought a near miracle during the early months after secession in raising, equipping, and training a formidable army. By August, 1861, the Confederacy had more than 200,000 men under arms, and the number was rising steadily. True, most of the weapons of the army had not been produced in the South; a majority of them had been seized in the United States arsenals and armories taken as various states withdrew from the Union. Only 10 per cent of the small arms borne by Southern troops during the first two years of the war were manufactured in the Confederacy, and the supply of weapons being purchased in Europe by ordnance agents came at first in a trickle. But for a people in the birth throes of nationhood—a predominantly agricultural people—so quickly to place in the field an army of this proportion was without precedent. Davis made no idle boast when in February, 1862, he said: "Our people have rallied with unexampled unanimity . . . with firm resolve to perpetuate by arms the right which they could not peacefully secure. A million of men, it is estimated, are now standing in hostile array, and waging war along a frontier of thousands of miles." With prodigious effort the South had girded herself for war.

The cause of Southern independence rested as much on the vitality of Confederate finance as of Confederate arms. Without the first, the second could not long endure. For this reason, some felt that Robert Toombs ought to be named to the critical post of Secretary of the Treasury. In the United States Senate Toombs had possessed the reputation of being an expert in finance. But Davis chose the impetuous Georgian to head the State Department instead, and the principle of geographic distribution in the appointment of cabinet members gave the Treasury position to South Carolina. This state's delegation at Montgomery recommended Christopher G. Memminger for the job, and Davis made the appointment. Memminger was a native of Germany who had been brought to America as a youth and had risen from a Charleston orphanage to become a lawyer of ability. He was known in South Carolina for his honesty and (paradoxically in view of his subsequent career in the Confederacy) for his hostility to paper money.

Memminger's task as Confederate Secretary of the Treasury was an impossible one. He was called upon to convert the non-liquid capital of an agrarian economy—primarily land, slaves, and one season's crop of cotton—into the immense fund of cash and credit required for the waging of total war. This was a challenge to baffle a William Pitt or an Alexander Hamilton, and Memminger was neither. His own lack of foresight was compounded by the fiscal ineptitude of the Congress and the impecuniousness and financial conservatism of the Southern people. A careful student of the epoch has written, "If I were asked what was the greatest single weakness of the Confederacy, I should say . . . that it was in this matter of finances."

But the Davis administration did strive to fashion a sound national financial system. Memminger was devoted, honest, and industrious. He sought the advice of leading Southern statesmen and financiers, and Davis trusted and supported him in the shaping of Confederate fiscal policy. The Treasury Department began in a Montgomery bank building in a room furnished out of the Secretary's own pocket. Initial expenses of the government were met with a loan of $500,000 from the state of Alabama; and presently the Treasury received somewhat more than this figure in coin seized in the United States mint and customhouse in New Orleans.

Memminger endeavored to finance the Confederacy with loans, taxes, and the cautious issue of treasury notes. But his initial measure of the wants of the infant republic was woefully short, for he dreamed of a peaceful regime with a minimum of government expense. Upon his recommendation, Congress voted in February, 1861, a bond issue of $15,000,000 bearing 8 per cent interest to be secured by a small export tax on cotton. The bonds were redeemable in ten years, or in five if the government should see fit to shorten the term. To provide money until the bonds could be marketed, $1,000,000 in treasury notes were issued. Anticipating the tactics of the "four-minute" men of World War I, Confederate agents traveled throughout the South, speaking in towns, villages, and courthouses, exhorting the people to subscribe bonds as a patriotic duty. Citizens were at first eager to purchase, but a desperate shortage of cash among the traditionally indebted planters slowed the sale and ultimately threatened to halt it altogether. Finally the banks came to the rescue, purchasing heavily of the bonds and encouraging individuals to do the same. By mid-October the entire amount of the loan had been subscribed.

The coming of war altered the outlook of the administration, though at first the true magnitude and duration of the conflict were not sensed. Memminger knew that the immense cost of modern war could not be borne by current taxes alone, but he wisely advocated a maximum taxation in order to provide a sound basis for loans and to discharge the principal and interest on the bonds as they became payable. In May, 1861, upon the Secretary's advice, Congress authorized a loan of $50,000,000 in twenty-year bonds, a direct war tax of $15,000,000, an import duty of 12½ per cent, and an additional $20,000,000 in treasury notes. Since the sale of the first bonds still lagged because of a shortage of money, the administration adopted an expedient to induce the planters to subscribe the second loan. This was the Produce Loan. Planters were permitted to pledge for the purchase of bonds the income from their yet unharvested crops. Under the zealous direction of the famous New Orleans publicist, Chief Commissioner J. D. B. De Bow, the Produce Loan at first appeared to be a success. Subscriptions ran from one-quarter to the whole of the planters' crops of cotton, sugar, tobacco, and rice, and President Davis confidently predicted that the entire issue of bonds would be pledged in cotton alone.

In August the Produce Loan was increased to $100,000,000. But by now the early optimism concerning this source of revenue had faded in the face of unforeseen obstacles. Planters were alarmed over the prospect of having no market for their produce, a threat made real by the Federal blockade and a self-imposed embargo on cotton that was supposed to cause England and France to come to the assistance of the South. Producers feared that they might be forced to sell at ruinous prices in order to honor their pledges to purchase bonds, and they were not quieted by Memminger's assurances to the contrary. Also, a more ominous situation was now apparent. Many Southerners showed little enthusiasm for long-term

Confederate bonds, thus indicating that confidence was low in the financial future of the Confederacy. This is an understandable weakness of all newborn nations, and especially those whose permanency is still in question. The Secretary was obliged to report to Congress in July that bonds could not be relied upon as an immediate resource, and that additional notes must be printed. The lawmakers accordingly authorized along with the expanded Produce Loan another $100,000,000 in paper currency.

Memminger's request for taxes was not ignored. Congress enacted as a part of the revenue measures of August, 1861, a war tax of one-half of 1 per cent on the value of slaves, real estate, merchandise, bank and other corporate stock, money at interest, and an additional list of luxury items. At year's end the financial fate of the Confederacy still lay in the balance. Success would rest upon the determination of the lawmakers to pursue a stern policy of taxation and the willingness and ability of the people to purchase the government's bonds. Any other course would lead to the quicksands of treasury notes and inflation.

The capital of the Confederacy did not long remain in Montgomery. From the beginning, Southern leaders had intended to locate the seat of government elsewhere. From among the many cities that offered themselves for this honor, Richmond was soon chosen by the Congress. The Virginia capital was not picked because of its strategic location; indeed, Davis opposed the selection because the city lay in the outer marches of the Confederacy and would be dangerously exposed to enemy attack. But his objections were overruled out of political expediency. Virginians would be affronted if the capital were not placed in the mother commonwealth of the South, argued the congressmen. This had been one of the prospects held out to Virginia when in the spring Stephens had been sent there to urge an immediate union with the Confederacy. The promise was honored, and on July 20, 1861, Congress took up business in the colonnaded state capitol designed by Thomas Jefferson. The Confederate government would remain here until the final moments of dissolution near the end of the war.

The Provisional Government was created to last for not more than a year, and in November, 1861, Davis and Stephens were elected President and Vice President of the Confederacy. At the same time, members were elected to the Senate and House of Representatives of the Confederate Congress, which now replaced the unicameral body that had served as both Constitutional Convention and Provisional Congress. In spite of the urging of Southern journalists and political leaders for a demonstration of strength at the polls, the election was listless. No rival candidates for the presidency and vice presidency appeared, and, notwithstanding the bolts of criticism already being shot at the administration by fiery Robert Barnwell Rhett, the electoral vote was unanimous. This possibly bespoke the general satisfaction of the Southern people with the Davis administration. Popular approval of the Chief Executive may also account for the apathy of the voters, since in the absence of other candidates, there was no cause to fear for his election. The editor of the Charleston *Courier* offered this explanation. Or, a rising martial spirit may have drawn interest away from political affairs; for the South was now alive with the movement of troops to the frontiers, and the story of Confederate victories during the summer, at Manassas in Virginia and Wilson's Creek in Missouri, was still on every tongue.

On February 22, 1862—the anniversary of George Washington's birth—Davis was inaugurated President of the Confederacy. The day in Richmond was as dreary as that of the Montgomery ceremony a year earlier had been bright. Standing in an icy drizzle beneath the statue of the first American President, the slender Mississippian reaffirmed his determination to lead the South to independence and his faith that her people would accept no less. He declared that like their Colonial ancestors, the Southern people were being forced to vindicate by arms the right to constitutional representative government. He spoke proudly of the strides taken by his administration in establishing a lasting republic, and he praised the citizens of the land for rising nobly to its defense. But the address also contained a somber note. Within the month, Confederate armies had been defeated on many fronts, and Davis honestly and solemnly said that the South had met with serious disasters. He therefore called upon the people for increased devotion to the cause of freedom and upon God for succor in the day of trial. The Confederacy was on the threshold of a new stage in its brief and turbulent career.

I V

The Opposition Takes Shape

Davis interpreted his election to the presidency as a vote of confidence on his policies and a sign of unanimity among the people of the South. He accordingly moved with renewed assurance to fashion the land into a true nation in arms. But the voices of discord were already rising about him, and a low and scattered murmur of opposition was soon discernible throughout the South. One of Davis' friends said that the Mississippian was found guilty even before he had a chance to do anything wrong. The South was destined to wage a struggle within herself almost as bitter as the one with the Northern foe.

This inner conflict received the spark of life from one of the leading architects of secession—Robert Barnwell Rhett of South Carolina. Rhett's critics said that in the blighting of his personal ambition lay the secret of a fierce animosity for the Davis administration. They pointed out that Rhett had yearned for the presidency of the Confederacy and had been cut to the quick by Davis' failure to name him to a foremost position in the cabinet. But Rhett cherished Southern independence as few men did; he hardly would have resorted to a conscious betrayal of it out of personal rancor. Sublime and boundless egotism combined with deep Southern patriotism to make him an implacable foe of the Confederate government. Rhett was convinced that he was the Messiah to lead the Southern people to freedom.

The militant South Carolinian—himself the antithesis of moderation—suspected the wisdom and motives of all Southern moderates. Davis had been elected Provisional President largely because he was considered to be of the moderate persuasion. Rhett was obsessed with the fear of "the dread spirit of reconstruction" among this group. This was his way of saying that he suspected moderates of hoping still for some form of reconciliation with the North. Rhett had for more than a decade devoted his life to the cause of Southern independence; this opportunity to achieve it must not be forfeited. If the elected officials erred or faltered, then Rhett would provide the light and strength to carry them to the goal. When Davis rejected Rhett's admonition, the South Carolinian turned in fury upon the administration.

Rhett spoke to the South through the columns of his son's newspaper, the Charleston *Mercury*, advocating an aggressive diplomatic and military policy. Recognition by England and France ought if possible to be secured by offering them commercial advantages; should this fail, then it must be coerced with an embargo on cotton and tobacco. The states of the North ought to be invaded immediately, urged Rhett, on the premise that an initial victory or two would spread demoralization there and induce recognition abroad.

The Opposition Takes Shape

By the summer of 1861, the defensive policy of the Confederate government was apparent. Rhett's disapproval mounted rapidly and soon spread to other aspects of the Davis administration. The President and his advisers lacked competence in the management of military affairs, and patriotism had yielded to favoritism and caprice in Richmond. Autumn found Rhett in open opposition to the Davis Provisional Government, though to preserve the appearance of Southern unanimity he forbore to oppose the Mississippian's candidacy for the presidency. The *Mercury* ignored the election. But a more ominous note crept gradually into its columns, warning of executive usurpation and unconstitutional designs. Readers were reminded that heads of state in wartime always incline to an insidious expansion of their power under the guise of military urgency. Other editorials charged Davis with trespassing upon the powers of Congress in his appointment of general officers. Thus, early in the war Rhett cast abroad the seed of a poisonous plant—the fear of military despotism at the hands of Jefferson Davis.

Rhett's imprecations were at first largely scorned. The press and people of the Confederacy responded to his alarms with indignant rebuttals and affirmations of faith in the administration. The Charleston *Courier*, edited by Davis supporter Richard Yeadon, took sharp issue with Rhett, and the South Carolina legislature passed with but a single dissenting vote a resolution of confidence in the "ability, integrity, and patriotism" of the men in the Provisional Government. Finally, the unanimous election of Davis to a full term as President gave proof of high regard among most of the citizens of the South.

The administration had up to this point sailed a gentle sea, for it had on the whole been successful, its efforts attended with stability at home and victory in the field. Adversity changed the outlook overnight.

In the winter and spring of 1862, the Confederacy was smitten flank, center, and rear. On February 8 a strong Union force stormed and captured Roanoke Island, guarding the entrances to Pamlico and Albemarle Sounds in North Carolina. Two days earlier Fort Henry on the Tennessee River had been captured by General U. S. Grant; and on the sixteenth Grant took Fort Donelson on the Cumberland River, with most of its garrison of fifteen thousand men. The western Confederate army commanded by General Albert Sidney Johnston was threatened with disaster. Johnston took a desperate decision; he withdrew into northern Mississippi in order to concentrate his forces below the Tennessee River for a decisive counterstroke. In early March, as Johnston fell back through Tennessee, the major Southern army west of the Mississippi River, commanded by General Earl Van Dorn, lost the battle of Pea Ridge in northwestern Arkansas. This destroyed the possibility of seizing Missouri for the Confederacy. Three weeks later Southern troops led by General Henry H. Sibley met defeat at Glorieta Pass, New Mexico Territory; Confederate hopes of expansion in the Southwest were gone. An angry cry of protest arose against these failures. On April 6 Johnston struck mightily at the Federal army under General U. S. Grant in the battle of Shiloh; but Johnston was killed, Grant reinforced, and the Confederates driven again into retreat. Less than a month later the city of New Orleans, greatest metropolis and port of the Confederacy, was captured by the intrepid Admiral David G. Farragut. The South was sorely wounded.

Popular confidence in the government faltered sharply at these reverses, and many who had been Davis' staunchest supporters fell away. A Confederate congressman spoke of the President's "incredible incompetency," and famed Dixie diarist Mary B. Chesnut said that in Columbia, South Carolina, she knew not a half-dozen men who did not feel that they were Davis' superior in every respect. Rhett's strictures lost all restraint as he charged the government with inefficiency and stupidity and demanded a complete change of men and measures.

Editors of the Richmond *Examiner*, Edward A. Pollard and John M. Daniel, now joined the chorus against Davis. Pollard possessed Rhett's power of vituperation, coupled with perhaps a greater tendency to assail the personal character and motives of the President and his advisers. In 1862 Pollard brought out a book entitled *The First Year of the War*. It was a clever diatribe against the government, disguised as a factual history of the conflict up to that time. Every reverse was attributed to Davis' incompetence. The Southern people, according to Pollard, had put forth an effort worthy of victory, "and nothing was wanting but wisdom, energy and capacity on the part of the government to have inaugurated another series of brilliant achievements. . . ." Davis had ignored the "wisdom of the people" (Pollard's euphemism for his own opinion), for "he [Davis] desired to signalize the infallibility of his own intellect in every measure of the revolution, and to identify, from motives of vanity, his own personal genius with every event and detail. . . ." Confederate generals had been hamstrung by the interference of the President,

. . . who, instead of attending to the civil affairs of the government and correcting the monstrous abuses that were daily pointed out . . . was unfortunately possessed with the vanity that he was a great military genius, and that it was necessary for him to dictate, from his cushioned seat in Richmond, the details of every campaign, and to conform every movement in the field to the invariable formula of *"the defensive policy."*

Davis could never for any consideration be induced to change his mind on a point "that might compromise him in respect of conceit or punctilio." The members of the Confederate cabinet were, according to Pollard, "intellectual pigmies."

With Rhett and Pollard setting the pace in their influential newspapers, a storm of criticism broke against the President and cabinet in the winter and spring of 1862. The Confederacy was in crisis.

Davis resolutely met the challenge. Declaring that God Almighty had seen fit to chasten the land with affliction, he set aside a day in February, 1862, for fasting, humiliation, and prayer. To Congress he expressed the hope that the people would be nerved by the winter's defeats to an indomitable defense of their independence; and he urged the supreme step in nationalizing the Southern war effort—the adoption of conscription.

The decision to conscript men into the Southern army was a momentous one, not lightly taken by the President and his counselors. Davis was aware that it was a measure without precedent in American history and that it would affront the spirit of individualism and state rights among many of the people. But the situation facing him seemed desperate; mighty forces of invasion were poised on the borders of the South, and the Confederate armies appeared on the brink of dissolution. The hazard appeared to justify the risk.

The course of events leading to this extremity was a curious one. Confederate morale had been wonderfully exalted during the summer of 1861 by the victory at Manassas. Southern superstitions regarding the martial ineptitude of the enemy seemed amply confirmed; one Rebel really could whip five—or was it ten?—Yankees. In the minds of many, the war was finished; for Lincoln would not be so foolish as to persist in an attempt to accomplish the now obviously impossible. If so, the citizens of the South would rise as one man to repel the invaders; and if their strength should honorably fail, then let the land be ravaged and the population annihilated before it submit to the "Black Abolitionists." Better death than serfdom!

This proud spirit of resistance was authentic; they were doubtless sincere who pledged blood and treasure to a defense of the soil and vowed to see it rather a blackened waste than a conquered province. But they failed to consider the weakness of the flesh. The initial outpouring of men into the Confederate army had volunteered for one year's service. Few doubted that the conflict would be won by then. Most of them had rushed headlong to the colors without regard to the welfare of families, businesses, or crops, and they were sorely needed at home to place affairs in order. Customary disillusionments of life in the ranks came on quickly. Existence in camp and field was often brutal, with rations, clothing, and shelter totally inadequate. Thousands of soldiers died the first year of pneumonia, measles, chicken pox, and other diseases. Apprehension spread in the South as the determination of the Northern government and people became apparent in the marshalling of their great armies. Then came repeated Confederate defeats in the field, followed by bitter denunciations of the competence and motives of the Confederate government. Morale of civilians and soldiers waned, and the armies were threatened with depletion as the twelve-month enlistment of many of the troops neared its end.

The Confederacy

The Provisional Congress had moved in December, 1861, to prevent this contingency. It provided a bounty of $50 and a furlough of sixty days to soldiers who would re-enlist for two or three years, or for the duration of the war. Re-enlisting troops were also given the privilege of reorganizing themselves into units as high as regiments and electing new officers. Later acts of Congress extended these privileges to new volunteers also. Results were disappointing. Volunteers came forward slowly, and large numbers of men already in service indicated their intention not to remain. Sterner measures were clearly in order.

On March 28, 1862, Davis asked Congress to conscript into the Confederate army for the duration of the war all men between the ages of eighteen and thirty-five who were eligible for military duty. He skirted the major reason for this request —the likely thinning of the armies—and said that conscription was necessary to the equitable distribution of the burden of military service. The prospect of hostile invasion had so animated the people of the South, he declared, that their offering of themselves must be regulated; youths under eighteen who required further instruction and men over thirty-five whose maturity was needed to maintain the domestic economy ought to be spared. In order to do this, all men of military age must be called to the ranks.

Among the leaders and spokesmen of the South sentiment was surprisingly strong in favor of so drastic and unprecedented a measure as conscription. Many who were otherwise at hopeless odds supported it. Rhett and Pollard, implacable critics of Davis, advocated conscription, as did the staunchest supporters of the administration. Generals Robert E. Lee and Joseph E. Johnston had for some time urged it. Congress passed the conscription act on April 16 by a vote of more than two to one.

But the conscription act brought into the open the deadliest conflict within the Confederacy, that of state rights as opposed to Southern nationalism. Unsettled in the Confederate organic law, this dangerous constitutional question had lain dormant during the first year of the Southern republic. Davis' nationalistic views had largely prevailed. The major instrument of the government—the army—had been formed as a national organization, though the advocates of state rights had looked on with apprehension. Governor John Milton of Florida in December, 1861, warned that the growing Confederate army with its reins in the hands of the central government threatened to "sap the very foundation of the rights of the states." The honeymoon of the centralists and the state rightists ended with the passage of the conscription act.

Among the first to denounce the act was Governor Joseph E. Brown of Georgia, soon to become the stormy petrel of state rights in the Confederacy. Brown was of humble origin, boasting that he "rose from the mass of the people." Born in South Carolina and reared in the mountainous western section of Georgia, he was one of a remarkable group of ante-bellum Southern political leaders who represented the "common people," or yeoman farmers and hill folk, as distinguished from the aristocratic planters. Brown was shrewd, puritanical, and obstinate. He believed with equal fervor in Southern independence and state rights, and he was never able to see that, at least for a time, state rights must be subordinated to the gaining of independence. From the beginning, Brown had been suspicious of a strong Confederate government; he now broke openly with the Davis administration.

The Confederacy

A week after the passage of the conscription act, Brown wrote the first of a series of letters to Davis bitterly denouncing the act as an illegal intrusion upon the rights of the states. Georgia would be stripped of the power to defend herself, he said. "I cannot consent to commit the state to a policy which is in my judgment subversive of her sovereignty and at war with all the principles for the support of which Georgia entered into this revolution." The act was a "bold and dangerous usurpation by Congress of the reserved rights of the states." Brown wrote to Vice President Stephens, "I entered into this revolution to contribute my humble mite to sustain the rights of the States and prevent the consolidation of Government, and I am still a rebel till this object is accomplished, no matter who may be in power." In public addresses and printed pamphlets Brown was even less restrained. Conscription violated the Constitution and bordered on military despotism, he charged. It would convert the free citizens of the state into chattels of the central government.

Brown was not alone in his opposition to conscription. Vice President Stephens, Robert Toombs (now a brigadier general in the Confederate army, but still an influential voice in the South), and many lesser figures shared Brown's views. Stephens questioned both the constitutionality and the wisdom of the act before it was passed. "Conscripts," he said, "will go into battle as a horse goes from home; volunteers, as a horse towards home: you may drive the latter hard and it does not hurt him." Thus the most urgent measure of the Confederate government to muster strength for a defense of the South was publicly challenged by leading figures of the Confederacy and entangled in bitter constitutional debate.

The Opposition Takes Shape

Even before the passage of the conscription act, Davis and a hostile minority in Congress were in conflict. Certain of the lawmakers lost all faith in the Chief Executive over the conduct of the war during the winter of 1862; the possibility of deposing him apparently was considered but abandoned. Instead, the administration was placed under severe attack, with Secretary of War Judah P. Benjamin as the primary target. Benjamin replaced Walker in the War Office during the previous summer and had the misfortune of being there at the moment of initial Confederate reverses in the field. The Southern press and Congress demanded a scapegoat; any incumbent would have been laid upon the rack.

Congressman Henry S. Foote of Tennessee led the assault against the Davis government. Foote was a turbulent and erratic politician whose path had crossed that of Davis before the war; in 1851 Foote had defeated Davis for the governorship of Mississippi. In the spring of 1862 Foote introduced bills of censure against Benjamin, one of which would have abolished the office of Secretary of War and replaced it with that of general in chief. These were undisguised blows at the administration. The bills were defeated, but they drew enough "yeas" to serve notice of a growing cleavage between the Chief Executive and a significant element in Congress.

The rift was never healed. Leaders of the antiadministration faction in Congress were Foote of Tennessee in the House of Representatives and Louis T. Wigfall, irrepressible Texas "fire-eater," in the Senate. By January, 1862, Vice President Stephens was in the ranks of the opposition. A constant drumfire of censure was directed against the President and his advisers and policies. As early as the summer of 1861, Congressman Lawrence M. Keitt of South Carolina had labeled the cabinet a "farce"; this body would remain the object of severe congressional criticism until the fall of the Confederacy.

Fortunately, Davis also had able supporters in Congress. Senators Benjamin Hill of Georgia and Robert Barnwell of South Carolina were powerful friends of the administration, as were Speaker of the House Thomas S. Bocock of Virginia and Representative Ethelbert Barksdale of Mississippi in the lower chamber. These men defended the President against the irresponsible tirades of Wigfall and Foote and gained passage of most of the measures vital to the Confederate cause. But they were never able to unite Congress closely behind the administration; the bitter feud endured and crippled the Southern war effort until the end.

V

Glow of Victory

Southern disasters of the winter and spring of 1862 suddenly gave way to a series of brilliant victories in the summer. Through conscription and volunteering, the Confederate armies were maintained; and Generals Robert E. Lee and Thomas J. "Stonewall" Jackson nerved their troops to a mighty effort that repeatedly sent the enemy columns northward in defeat. Southern hearts were fired by news of Jackson's successes in the Shenandoah Valley, the repulse of McClellan's great army before the gates of Richmond, and Lee's triumph at Second Manassas. Rhett retired to the management of his South Carolina plantations, and the voices of the opposition were momentarily quiet. The Lord had answered the prayers of his children, thought the South. This was the Confederacy's hour of glory.

These triumphs were accompanied by important developments within the Confederacy. In March, Davis had named his cabinet. Brought over from the provisional cabinet were

The Confederacy

Postmaster General Reagan, Secretary of the Navy Mallory, and Secretary of the Treasury Memminger. Thomas H. Watts of Alabama was appointed Attorney General. There were two significant changes; a new Secretary of War was appointed, and Benjamin was made Secretary of State.

In transferring Benjamin from War to State, Davis bowed to the will of the hostile faction in Congress and at the same time reaffirmed his own faith in his appointee. Benjamin was the storm center of the administration. His conduct as Secretary of War was creditable; he had done everything within his power to expand and equip the armies of the South, and, considering the limited facilities at hand, had done well. He nevertheless became increasingly unpopular with the Congress, the press, and the people of the Confederacy. Many people disliked Benjamin because he was a Jew; many others disliked him because of his unruffled suavity. Perhaps some envied his keen intelligence. Unfortunate altercations arose between Benjamin and prominent Confederate generals. He differed with Joseph E. Johnston over the issuing of furloughs to the soldiers. A sharp letter to P. G. T. Beauregard ruffled the Creole's sensibilities. When, upon Davis' instructions, Benjamin ordered troops withdrawn from a position selected by Stonewall Jackson, the dour Presbyterian warrior promptly offered his resignation. Jackson was placated and kept with his command; Benjamin's prestige suffered from the incident. Finally, Confederate failures in the field were laid at Benjamin's door.

This was transparently unjust. Davis and the commanders appointed by him made the dispositions and strategic decisions that preceded these defeats. But the Chief Executive was beyond the immediate reach of his enemies in Congress; they struck at him by attacking Benjamin. Seeing that the Senate would not approve the appointment of Benjamin as Secretary of War, Davis selected for that position George Wythe Randolph of Virginia.

Randolph was popular with the press and with those citizens who knew him; he was a grandson of Thomas Jefferson and had been one of Virginia's leading advocates of secession. He had the good fortune to serve in the War Office during the period of brightest Confederate success—the summer of 1862. For months Randolph played a passive role in his office, leading the well-known diarist of the department, John B. Jones, to say that Randolph was a mere clerk. But Randolph made one important contribution to the Southern victories that occurred during his incumbency; he interpreted the conscription act stringently and administered it with vigor. His orders were to enforce the law "with the utmost activity, and without fear, favor, or affection."

This act probably saved the Confederacy in the spring of 1862. Its most significant results were indirect, for it did not at once bring into the army a great number of men. But it held in service the thousands of twelve-month volunteers, now seasoned troops, who had previously shown an intention of returning to their homes. Also, it stimulated a vast increase in volunteering, for it gave to military organizations then being formed a thirty-day period of grace in which to fill their ranks. Thousands of young Southerners escaped the stigma of conscription by enrolling in these units at this time. Had there been no conscription, many of the twelve-month soldiers probably in time would have returned to the colors, and many of the volunteers would have come forward. These men fought too steadfastly in the arduous campaigns of the next three years for their courage or patriotism to be questioned. But they

The Confederacy

would have come at their leisure, when all at home seemed right for them to leave. With the vast forces of McClellan in the east and Halleck in the west pressing upon the South, any weakening of the armies at that moment would have been fatal. Instead, Lee and Jackson were provided with the strength for their victories of the summer.

While the armies of the South maneuvered and fought to hold the invaders at bay, her leaders groped desperately for the means to sustain the military effort and the domestic economy. This proved more difficult than winning battles in the field. Severed by war from the customary markets and sources of manufactured goods in the North, the Confederacy strove for the greatest possible measure of self-sufficiency. She was never able to throw off her dependence on Europe for many of the weapons of war and goods of civilian use, but some of the most remarkable achievements of the epoch were made in the attempt.

The South was rich in industrial raw materials. If these could be converted into finished products, the dangerous and costly reliance on outsiders would be ended. Coal and iron ore abounded in portions of Virginia, North Carolina, Tennessee, Georgia, and Alabama. Lead was found in Virginia, Tennessee, and Arkansas. Wool was grown in Texas and many other parts of the South. A thriving cattle industry throughout the Confederacy, and especially in Texas and Louisiana, provided hides for an ample supply of leather. Cotton was the distinguishing staple of the region. Industry had not shunned the ante-bellum South for want of resources. Her leaders now set about to do overnight what they and their fathers had failed to do in more than two centuries—industrialize the South.

The Confederate government stimulated the expansion of

industry by lending money to private enterprisers. Congress authorized loans up to one-half the cost of establishing new industries or enlarging old ones. Goods had to be sold to the Confederacy at prices set by the government, and controls were exercised through the withholding of laborers and raw materials. These measures had much of the desired effect. Factories sprang up throughout the Confederacy and the output of manufactured goods multiplied many fold.

The Tredegar Iron Works of Richmond remained the greatest of all Southern factories; it was the industrial heart of the Confederacy. Quite possibly the tenacity of Confederate authorities in fighting for Richmond was stiffened as much by the need for holding the Tredegar Works as for protecting the seat of government. The wartime experience of this great plant is worthy of a saga. Under the brilliant direction of the owner, Brigadier General Joseph R. Anderson, the Tredegar Works became the "mother" arsenal of the South, pouring forth in abundance the varied tools and weapons of industrialized warfare. Plating for the first American ironclad warship originated here. Nearly eleven hundred cannon employed by Southern forces on field and sea were made here. Much of the machinery for the other new-founded arsenals of the Confederacy was fashioned by the Tredegar Works. The great plant also served as a laboratory for making new and unusual weapons; it built the first submarine and the first torpedoes with which the Confederates vainly opposed the Federal navy.

Expansion of the Tredegar Works and conversion to military production exemplified the methods applied to the forced growth of Southern industry during the war. When the construction of cannon was threatened for want of pig iron, the Confederate government lent Anderson $500,000 for the purchase of coal mines and blast furnaces in order that he might supply his own crude metal. Mechanics and iron founders were detailed from the army to labor in the Tredegar Works and its subsidiaries. As before the war, hundreds of slaves served the foundries and shops. As the problem of securing laborers grew increasingly acute, Anderson reluctantly turned to the employment of Negro convicts from state penal institutions. Feeding the 2,500 workers and their families was a monumental task; the resourceful proprietor sent agents through Tennessee, North and South Carolina, Georgia, and Alabama to purchase corn, rice, and bacon for this purpose. When Confederate paper money was no longer acceptable to the farmers, Anderson bartered for necessities with nails, spikes, and bar iron. To clothe his laborers, Anderson built his own tannery and shoe factory and purchased blockade-runners that carried cotton to Bermuda and returned with the needed cloth. Through the countless vicissitudes of victory, invasion, and defeat the Tredegar Works never faltered; not until April 3, 1865, as the Confederates abandoned their capital, did its mills grow silent.

An equally spectacular development in Confederate manufacturing was that of the government-owned munitions and armaments plants. The hero of this accomplishment was the unpretentious Chief of Confederate Ordnance, General Josiah Gorgas. Gorgas was a native of Pennsylvania and a graduate of the United States Military Academy. Married to an Alabama woman, he had long identified himself with the cause of the South and had resigned from the United States army in order to join the forces of the Confederacy. In April, 1861, Gorgas was made head of the Ordnance Bureau; this was a singularly fortunate choice, for he soon proved himself an indefatigable worker and a genius of industrial organization. Under his inspiration, a remarkable arms and munitions industry sprang up in the South. Arsenals for the fashioning of artillery, small arms, and ammunition were established by the Confederate government in Richmond, Atlanta, Selma, and a dozen other cities across the land. By late 1862, these factories were in steady production; during the last two years of the war they were the major source of supply for the beleaguered South. A biographer has with justice said of Gorgas that he contributed more than any other man, with the exception of Robert E. Lee, to the strength of the Confederate armies. "The world has hardly seen such a miraculous transformation of ploughshares into swords."

In the wake of this wartime expansion of manufacturing came a rising popular enthusiasm over the prospect of an industrial postwar South. Presently the Manufacturing and Direct Trade Association of the Confederate States was organized, with the famed ante-bellum Southern factory master, William Gregg, as president. Editors everywhere hailed the burgeoning mines and factories as harbingers of a self-sufficient South. Chattanooga became to her citizens the "Pittsburgh of the South"; other communities took on similar titles.

As the stern exigencies of war awakened the industries of the South, they also sharply altered her agricultural ways. In peacetime the planters of the area had purchased from the farmers of the Northwest much of the required foodstuffs, such as corn, flour, pork, and beef, in order that a maximum portion of the land could be devoted to the great commercial crops. Secession had cut off this source of supply, and the growing effectiveness of the Northern blockade threatened to sever all others. Faced with this extremity, the Confederacy set about to feed herself. Crops of cotton, tobacco, sugar, and rice were already planted in the spring of 1861 when the war came, and the ensuing harvest was heavy in all of them. Four and one-half million bales of cotton were ginned that fall, and the yield of sugar was far greater than ever before. But the following winter the Southern press took up the cry for a reduction of acreage in the staples and a corresponding increase in the planting of corn and other subsistence crops. Cotton could be blockaded and rendered useless, said the editors, but corn, wheat, and livestock would make the South invulnerable. "Food would win the war!"

To large numbers of planters and farmers this logic was convincing. During the winter they held mass meetings in their schoolhouses and courthouses, and resolved to plant from one-third to one-half less cotton than usual in the spring. Not content with voluntary crop reduction, most state governments limited by law the growing of traditional Southern staples. The permissible amount of cotton varied from state to state, from one to three acres per hand; in Virginia a comparable limit was placed on the planting of tobacco. Congress pondered a uniform restriction for the entire Confederacy but finally abandoned the idea as unconstitutional.

In the spring of 1862 landowners of the South practiced crop reduction and conversion to foodstuffs with remarkable fidelity, considering that restrictions were still voluntary. Public sentiment strongly supported these measures as a patriotic duty, and in some instances committees of safety were formed to bring reluctant planters into line. The 1862 cotton yield was only one-third that of the previous season. This was not altogether the result of voluntary action on the part of the Southern people, for by now some of the land was in the hands of the enemy. But the heart of the Cotton Kingdom still belonged to the Confederacy, and the sharp decrease in the growing of the great staple was caused primarily by the shift to other crops.

Although the Confederacy took great strides toward industrial and agricultural independence, the problem of national finance grew ever more vexing. An abiding reluctance among the people to purchase government bonds threatened the Treasury with bankruptcy. Some method must be found to convert bonds into money, else both the domestic economy and the war effort would collapse. Planters who under the Produce Loan had pledged the income of their 1861 crops to the purchase of bonds now clamored for the Treasury to accept in payment the produce itself. If this should be done at a price fixed by the government—a favorable one, it was hoped—they would no longer be subject to the vagaries of the local market. In other words, the planters wished to trade cotton for bonds instead of selling it at market price and then paying cash for the bonds.

At the same time the difficulty of raising money in the Confederacy caused Memminger to turn his eyes to Europe as a source of funds. Cotton could be used there, he reasoned, as security for loans. In the spring of 1862, he recommended to Congress that produce be accepted in exchange for bonds, thus meeting in one stroke the demands of the planters and the need of the government for cotton. This was approved in April by the lawmakers, along with another $165,000,000 in bonds bearing 8 per cent interest, to mature in thirty years. The Confederacy acquired hundreds of thousands of bales of cotton in this manner.

Meantime, the Confederacy drifted dangerously toward inflation. During the first year the government lived principally on paper currency. Memminger was not at first alarmed. In the spring of 1862 he recommended and Congress approved an additional issue of $50,000,000 in treasury notes. This optimism was ill-founded. For the effects of the war tax enacted the previous August were bitterly disappointing. Most of the states assumed the burden of the tax for their citizens, as the law permitted, and instead of raising the money by taxation, the states borrowed it by issuing their own bonds. At the same time, in order to ease the strain of purchasing state bonds, they made heavy issues of state treasury notes. Thus, Confederate notes returning to the Confederate Treasury in taxes were replaced by state notes. As the year 1862 progressed, the price of food and other commodities rose swiftly, buoyed by increased government purchases, a severe shortage of goods, and a plethora of state and Confederate paper. The rise in prices accelerated the drain on the Confederate Treasury; before summer's end Memminger reported requisitions of $28,000,000 that could not be met, and declared that more than $200,000,-000 would be required before January, 1863, to support the war. Congress in desperation turned again to the printing press, authorizing in October the issue of more than $140,000,000 in notes.

Memminger was now thoroughly alarmed. Warning of depreciation and disaster, he called upon Congress to reduce the amount of notes in circulation by causing them to be funded (exchanged for bonds redeemable in the future) and by laying a heavy tax on personal incomes. Congress weakly shunned the tax, but in October passed a funding act providing for the exchange of treasury notes for 8 per cent bonds until December 1, 1862. After this date the notes could be exchanged only for 7 per cent bonds. Effects of the act were negligible. More rapidly than the old notes could be withdrawn, new ones had to be issued to meet the voracious demands of war. Memminger in December, 1862, swallowed his fear and asked Congress for authority to issue another $200,000,000 in treasury notes. The only remedy at hand for the mortal illness of inflation was more inflation.

But the Southern mind was not primarily concerned during the summer and fall of 1862 with the vexations of finance. Victory was in the air. Lee's army was invincible. Soon the nations of Europe would recognize the new republic, and Lincoln and his minions would admit failure and leave the South in peace. A final demonstration of military prowess would convince the North and the world of the permanency of the Confederacy. With these hopes before him, Davis awaited the outcome of a great triple counteroffensive planned by his generals to free the South of invaders even to the frontier of her dreams. General Earl Van Dorn was to destroy the Federal forces lodged in upper Mississippi; General Braxton Bragg was to retake Kentucky; and General Lee was to liberate Maryland. Southern morale was high as on September 5 Lee's Army of Northern Virginia first crossed the Potomac.

VI

Shadow of Defeat

Victory beguiled the Southern mind during the summer of 1862 and veiled the latent discord within the Confederacy. Addressing the Congress in August, shortly after the repulse of McClellan's army at Richmond and on the eve of the great Confederate victory at Second Manassas, Davis said with sincerity:

> Our Army has not faltered in any of the various trials to which it has been subjected, and the great body of the people has continued to manifest a zeal and unanimity which not only cheer the battle-stained soldier, but give assurance to the friends of constitutional liberty of our final triumph in the pending struggle against despotic usurpation.

The nationalized war effort appeared to have brought independence within reach.

But the forces of dissent had not been destroyed; they were merely held in check. Indeed, they had continued to vex the Davis administration even during its most auspicious season, though with reduced vehemence. A favorite subject of censure was the secrecy of the government. This criticism was justified; the President often failed to take Congress and the people into his confidence, and Congress frequently debated and enacted important legislation behind closed doors. Long after Davis had sent agents to Europe for the purchase of military supplies he was attacked in the Charleston *Mercury* for failing to do so. It had not occurred to him to inform the country of such measures. A keen analyst of Davis' character has written that a "fireside chat" by him would have been inconceivable.

Pollard in the Richmond *Examiner* condemned with ardor the secret sessions of Congress, and certain influential members of that body supported the critical editor's view. Representative Foote, irrepressible foe of the administration whatever the issue, bitterly opposed congressional secrecy. William L. Yancey was the most determined critic of the closed door in the Senate. Addressing his colleagues in August, 1862, the famous orator convincingly argued that there was no cause to fear open debate on all issues, or the publication of the vote of individual members of the chamber. On the contrary, said Yancey,

The great public sentiment of our people today is of higher cast of revolutionary energy, wisdom and devotion than that of their government. And the only fear Senators need entertain of the effect of giving publicity to their proceedings is, that there will be a stern demand that they eschew all reliance for success other than upon their constituency, and that they shall call more freely for men and means to carry this war into the enemy's country. . . . In the Convention which framed the [United States] Constitution, Colonel Mason, of Virginia, said: "The people will not give their confidence to a secret journal—to the intrigues and factions naturally incident to secrecy."

The Confederacy

Secrecy nevertheless continued to prevail in the Confederate government—an increasing source of suspicion and malaise among the people.

Other measures considered by the President and Congress essential to the defense of the land aroused resentment and distrust among many Southerners. One of the chief of these was the suspension of the privilege of the writ of habeas corpus, an action made necessary by the turmoil arising in areas invaded or threatened by the Federal army. In February, 1862, immediately after the loss of Fort Donelson, Congress authorized the President to suspend the privilege of the writ and declare martial law in towns and districts menaced by the enemy. Suspension of the writ was a common practice in war, one often resorted to by the Lincoln government, but it keenly affronted the Southern sense of individual and local rights. It was looked upon by many as a dangerous encroachment of the central government upon the authority of the states. Davis discerned this anxiety, and exercised with profound caution the power granted him in the act.

Though used sparingly, the habeas corpus act soon was an abomination to the people. On the eve of Federal invasion, Davis suspended the writ in New Orleans to enable General Mansfield Lovell to preserve the city from chaos. From Louisiana and elsewhere in the Confederacy arose a bitter protest. Richmond was placed under martial law and purged of spies, traitors, and gamblers by the military governor, General John H. Winder. Winder's methods were insolent and despotic; they vastly intensified the loathing of the Southern people for martial law. Alarmed at the popular revulsion, Congress curtailed the President's power to withhold the writ. Davis subsequently invoked the act temporarily in portions of North and South Carolina, but forbore to do so in other areas where it was needed.

More disturbing than the presidential use of martial law was the proclamation of it by certain commanders in the field. To curb the civil disorder and defection that came in the wake of Federal invasion, Confederate generals in the summer of 1862 placed large portions of Arkansas, Louisiana, and Mississippi under martial law. General Braxton Bragg did the same for Atlanta. Powerful voices of reprobation were immediately raised throughout the South, including those of many former friends of the administration. To the enemies of the government, the imposition of martial law was but another step in the direction of tyranny. The most vehement of critics were the Georgia triumvirate of Davis' opponents. Vice President Stephens denounced Bragg's action in Atlanta as being unconstitutional; Governor Joseph E. Brown declared it a subversion of the government and sovereignty of the state; and fractious Brigadier General Robert Toombs wrote: "Davis and his Jannissaries—the regular army—conspire for the destruction of all who will not bend to them, and avail themselves of the public danger to aid them in their selfish and infamous schemes." Led by Foote, the hostile wing of Congress heaped coals of wrath upon the President and his generals for their application of the act.

Opposition came to a head in the spring of 1863 when Representative Ethelbert Barksdale of Mississippi offered a bill empowering the President to suspend the writ at his discretion in any part of the Confederacy. Though the real purpose of this bill was known to be the enforcement of the conscription act and the curbing of Unionist activities, it was bitterly assailed as a menace to the constitutional liberty of all Southerners. Thus the foes of conscription cleverly drew support from many advocates of conscription in opposing the most effective act for enforcing it. Foote and others told lurid tales of the oppression of humble citizens by heartless military commanders, and the Barksdale bill was defeated. The Charleston *Mercury* expressed its satisfaction over the result, but solemnly warned readers to guard against renewed attempts to erect a military despotism.

But the most ominous controversy of all was that over the relationship between the Confederacy and her constituent parts—state rights as opposed to national authority. For as the conflict grew in intensity, so did the pressure of the Confederate government upon the several states for centralized control of the full resources of the South. This effort affronted the deep state-rights consciousness of many Southern leaders, who feared Confederate nationalism as much as they had that of the United States, and resistance to centralization rose in proportion to the pressure exerted in its behalf.

Early in the war every Southern state government had formed its own army for local defense, with the result that scores of thousands of men and vast quantities of arms and equipment were held out of Confederate service. The strength of these local military forces by spring 1862 varied from five to ten thousand men each. Southern military strategy was crippled by the insistence of state governors on the scattering of Confederate troops around the entire perimeter of the South, thus impairing the ability of the administration to concentrate its forces at critical points for decisive strokes against the enemy. General Albert Sidney Johnston strove futilely in the winter 1861/62 to accomplish such a concentration for the defense of the Mississippi Valley. Only at the last desperate hour, after the loss of Forts Henry and Donelson, was General Braxton Bragg with his well-trained force of ten thousand men ordered from Mobile and Pensacola to the support of Johnston's depleted army at Corinth, Mississippi. This junction made possible the Confederate counteroffensive at Shiloh, in which the Union army barely escaped destruction. A few thousand additional Confederate soldiers would have made victory certain; it has been estimated that at this time more than 100,000 troops were standing idle in state military formations throughout the Confederacy.

The conscription act of April, 1862, was in part designed to bring into the Confederate service these large numbers of state troops, and it would have done so if it had been fully supported by the state governments. But from the beginning it was not supported. Hardly a governor gave unqualified cooperation in the enforcement of the act. Instead, they began at once to find ways of evading it in order to maintain their own military forces and civil services. Sections of the act providing for the exemption of necessary state officials were seized upon as a means of nullifying it or reducing its effectiveness to the minimum. Governor Brown of Georgia was the arch obstructionist; with unsurpassed cunning he sought to render it meaningless in his state. Brown declared exempt all sheriffs, deputies, clerks, magistrates, notaries public, tax collectors, and state militia officers and was thus able to hold thousands of able-bodied men of military age out of the Confederate army. Most of the other Southern governors, though less outspoken in their resistance to the administration, followed a course of action quite like that of Brown. In spite of the vigorous application of the conscription act during the summer of 1862 by Secretary of War Randolph, it fell lamentably short of mustering the full strength of the South into the service of the Confederacy.

Had the prospect of early triumph remained undimmed, Davis probably could have curbed the centrifugal forces that were dissipating the energies of the South. Southern national consciousness and esprit de corps rose during the summer of 1862 with every success in the field. But the wine of victory was soon spent. An overture of liberation from Lee to the people of Maryland fell upon deaf ears, and on September 17 the Union army under McClellan attacked the Confederates at Sharpsburg with fury and superior numbers. McClellan moved with assurance, for he had been providentially warned of Lee's plans by the capture of a copy of his orders. The assault was beaten off through Lee's sterling leadership and the courage of his troops. Nevertheless, the campaign and the strategic initiative were lost; Lee was forced to withdraw into Virginia and await the renewal of the Federal offensive.

Two weeks later Van Dorn struck fiercely at the Northern army under General Rosecrans at Corinth, Mississippi; but the Confederates were bloodily repulsed.

Meanwhile, Bragg marched north from Tennessee with Louisville as his objective. He outpaced his adversary, General Buell, and had the prize within his grasp; then he faltered and for a week became absorbed in political affairs, issuing a futile invitation to the states of the agrarian Northwest to join the Confederacy in a war against the industrial East, and leaving his army in order to attend the inauguration of a "Confederate" governor of Kentucky who had accompanied him from Tennessee. On October 8 the rival forces met in the battle of Perryville. Like Sharpsburg, this contest was a tactical victory but a strategic defeat for the Confederacy; Bragg was obliged to retreat into Tennessee and resume the defensive.

The Confederate triple counteroffensive was dead.

These reverses spread demoralization throughout the South and crippled the prestige of the administration. Davis himself was quoted at the time as saying that the Confederacy was in her darkest hour; that she had put forth her full strength without decisive result, while the enemy was yet unextended. Many Southerners began to doubt the ability of the Confederacy to win the war.

At this moment of defeat in the field and despondency among the people, the Davis administration was further weakened by a rift within itself. Early in November, Secretary of War Randolph suddenly resigned his position. The immediate cause of the resignation was a sharp note from Davis in effect reprimanding the Secretary for changing the orders of a commander in the field without securing the President's approval. The circumstances were as follows: General John C. Pemberton, commander of the Mississippi Department, was under siege by General William T. Sherman in the city of Vicksburg. In an effort to bring reinforcements to Pemberton, and hoping to achieve a more effective concentration of arms for the defense of the lower Mississippi Valley, Randolph instructed General Theophilus Holmes, commander of the Trans-Mississippi Department, to cross the river in order to co-operate with Pemberton. Davis was not consulted in this decision, though he was informed of it after the letter was sent to Holmes. Davis immediately wrote the Secretary that this was a mistake, that it was essential for each commander to remain within his own department. Furthermore, such actions could be taken only with the President's authorization; all communications to generals must be sent through the Adjutant General's office, and the President must be consulted in the appointment of every commanding officer and the movement of all troops. Randolph asked whether these instructions were meant literally. Davis answered yes, though he explained that by the movement of troops he had really meant the designation of departments and the transfer of arms. Stung by what he considered an intent to reduce him to the level of a clerk, Randolph peremptorily withdrew from the cabinet.

Davis unquestionably was right in insisting that he decide issues of strategy and the disposition of forces. But Randolph was right in attempting to concentrate the scattered armies of the western Confederacy for a decisive blow at the invaders. Davis never seemed to grasp this principle, but continued to regard the various departmental lines as sacrosanct, not to be crossed even to save an army from destruction or a key fortress from capture.

Presently Davis appointed James Alexander Seddon to the position recently left vacant by Randolph. Seddon was a frail and cadaverous man whose portrait—taken in a yamilke-like black cap—more nearly resembled a pensive Jewish rabbi than a man of war. To choleric Rebel war clerk Jones, Seddon looked like "an exhumed corpse after a month's interment." The new Secretary was a Virginia planter and aristocrat; he had been one of the leaders of secession in his state. He possessed one rare advantage; he was a close friend of Jefferson Davis and at the same time a favorite of two of Davis' most implacable critics, Pollard of the Richmond *Examiner* and Rhett of the Charleston *Mercury*. Seddon belied his looks; he was a man of energy and imagination, and he ultimately influenced the military strategy of the Confederacy more than any other member of the government, save the President.

Seddon analyzed with keen insight the weakness of the Southern military position; Lee's army barred the eastern routes of invasion, but in the west the Federal columns were thrusting for the vitals of the Confederacy. A capable general must be selected for the west and given full power to co-ordinate the desultory efforts of the forces in that area. Nowhere was Seddon's influence with the President more strikingly shown than in the naming of this commander. His choice was Joseph E. Johnston, who for months since the defense of Richmond in the Peninsular campaign had been idle, nursing his wounds and his pride. Davis had little faith in Johnston, nor did Judah P. Benjamin, the President's most intimate friend and counselor. Seddon nevertheless prevailed, and on November 24 Davis reluctantly signed the order creating a theater of operations between the Appalachian Mountains and the Mississippi River, with Johnston in command. The result was bitterly disappointing. Davis and Johnston caviled endlessly over the precise nature of Johnston's orders. Johnston refused or was unable to exercise full authority in co-ordinating the western armies, and in the end nothing of significance came out of the new command.

The winter 1862/63 and the following spring brought the Confederacy her greatest victories. Twice the Union army pressed south toward the Southern capital. Twice it was severely beaten, first at Fredericksburg (December 13) and then at Chancellorsville (May 1–4). Lee and Jackson had confirmed their genius, and the Army of Northern Virginia its fortitude. But "Mighty Stonewall" fell at Chancellorsville and the South was filled with sorrow even as her hopes were rekindled by success. Chastened by grief and exalted by victory, the Southern people braced to a still greater effort and sacrifice.

Smiting of the Federal offensive at Chancellorsville in early May gave respite to the South, and again for a moment her leaders held the strategic initiative in the east. Seddon was still primarily concerned with the faltering armies beyond the Appalachians. On December 31 the forces of Bragg and Rosecrans had met in the battle of Murfreesboro, thirty miles southeast of Nashville. After two days of costly and indecisive combat Bragg had withdrawn. Now he was falling back upon Chattanooga, with Rosecrans pressing after him; the important Tennessee rail center was in grave danger of capture. Meantime, on the Mississippi River, Grant was closing the trap around Vicksburg, a position that could not now be reinforced from beyond the Mississippi, since the only Southern army capable of doing so had been smashed in December, 1862, in the battle of Prairie Grove, Arkansas. The double dissection of the Confederacy was well under way. Seddon planned a bold move to redress the balance in the west; Lee would hold in check the defeated and passive Union army facing him, at the same time sending a portion of his troops to join those of the lower Mississippi Valley in a decisive stroke against Grant. Lee objected, proposing instead to relieve pressure on the west by carrying the war to the enemy. Davis upheld Lee, and Seddon was dissuaded from his plan; the west remained the thinly manned and vulnerable rampart of the Confederacy.

On June 15 Lee's tattered veterans began marching north, crossing the Potomac. A great Southern victory on enemy

Ruins in Fredericksburg, Virginia, showing houses destroyed
by bombardment in December, 1862

Destruction of Southern rolling mill and Hood's ordnance train.
Photograph by G. N. Barnard, 1864

Southern women sewing clothing. "Industry of ladies in clothing the
soldiers, and zeal in urging their beaux to go to the war"
(The Bettmann Archive)

soil might yet draw off the Union forces pressing upon Chattanooga and Vicksburg and induce the nations of Europe to give succor to the beleaguered Confederacy. This hope was short-lived. On July 1–3 the hosts of Lee and Meade met on the deadly field of Gettysburg; Lee's assaults were broken and the gray army recoiled, defeated and crippled, into Virginia. It would not again venture beyond the borders of this state. The day after Gettysburg brought still another disaster to Southern arms in the surrender of Vicksburg and its defenders. The tide of the Confederacy was in the ebb.

Victory and defeat between autumn 1862 and the following summer taxed the resources of the South beyond all previous exigency and spurred the Confederate government to draw into its service a fuller measure of the men and materials of the land. Ten days after the battle of Sharpsburg, Congress passed the second conscription act, authorizing the President to call out men up to forty-five years of age.

This act intensified the old friction between Confederate and state authorities over the control of Southern manpower. Anticipating state hostility, Davis besought the various governors to support the more sweeping policy of conscription and to aid in arresting those who attempted to evade it. He went in person to Mississippi where he appealed to the legislature for its indorsement of the act. Friends of the administration in Congress did the same before the lawmaking bodies of their respective states. Nor did support come from friends alone; some of the bitterest critics of Davis joined in the effort to make the act acceptable. Senator William L. Yancey, addressing the Alabama legislature in favor of the measure, delivered a powerful discourse on the need for centralized control of all the South's military resources; and the Charleston *Mercury* and Richmond *Examiner* supported the new law with their influence.

The opposition was just as determined to render the act powerless. Notwithstanding that the Supreme Court of Georgia had ruled the first conscription act legal, Governor Brown now declared that the second measure should not be enforced in his state until it had been sanctioned by the legislature. Vice President Stephens again denounced the principle of conscription. Senator Benjamin H. Hill, unswerving supporter of the administration, pled with the Georgia lawmakers to approve the law, and to the bitter disappointment of Brown and Stephens they did so. Brown then resumed his customary tactics of obstruction in order to cripple conscription in Georgia.

Late in 1862 Brown gained a powerful ally in the election of Zebulon Vance as Governor of North Carolina. Vance, like Brown, was sprung from the Southern yeomanry and considered himself a champion of the common folk. A conservative and Unionist before the war, he had supported Bell and Everett in the presidential campaign of 1860. But Vance shared the belief of most Southern Unionists in the abstract legality of secession, and Lincoln's call for troops converted Vance into an active separatist. He pledged himself in the race for the governorship to a full prosecution of the war, and though he received the votes of the North Carolina Unionists because of his earlier record of conservatism, he was faithful to the campaign promise. He was profoundly devoted to the cause of Southern independence but just as sincerely dedicated to the principle of state rights; and he believed that the war could be more effectively waged through state than through

Confederate control of the resources of the South. Vance soon took his place beside Brown as an implacable opponent of conscription and the centralized war effort.

The second conscription act contained a provision that excused from involuntary service the owners or overseers of plantations with as many as twenty Negro slaves. This measure was passed in the belief that it was needed in order to assure decorum among the Negroes and maximum production on the plantations. But it wreaked great mischief upon Southern morale and provided an easy target for those who opposed the principle of conscription. The law was vehemently denounced by the small farmers of the hill and piney woods areas of the South as discriminatory class legislation. It was grist for the mills of Brown and Vance.

Desertion thinned the Confederate ranks during the fall and winter of 1862 in the wake of reverses in the field and resentment over the new conscription law. The mountains of eastern Tennessee and western North Carolina and the hill country of Georgia, Alabama, and Mississippi teemed with shirkers and deserters formed into shotgun squads that boldly defied and sometimes killed the conscription officers. Davis traversed the South in December, urging a renewed faith in ultimate victory and explaining the necessity of exempting slaveowners or overseers from military service. He denied any intention of favoring the rich and declared that they bore their share of the burden of war; and he pointed to countless affluent planters and their sons in uniform and to others who wore souvenirs of combat in the form of empty sleeves, lamed figures, or marred features. Many of his hearers were convinced by these arguments, but many were not. To those who doubted, the "twenty nigger" law had converted the struggle for independence into a "rich man's war and a poor man's fight."

The victories of Fredericksburg and Chancellorsville stiffened the flagging spirit of the Southern people and a majority of them accepted Davis' explanations regarding the exemption of slaveowners. But a more insidious and dispiriting influence was abroad in the land; one that the government was incapable of curbing. Inflation was sapping the morale of the South. The quickening of military activities in the winter of 1862 and spring of 1863 bore heavily upon an empty treasury, and Memminger resigned himself to an endless issue of treasury notes. Congress in March authorized an additional $50,000,000 a month of this dangerous medium to meet the rising costs of war. In an effort to prevent the inflation that must normally follow an increase in paper currency, a second provision was adopted for funding outstanding notes.

Financial distress drove Memminger to an unprecedented step, a resort to the tax in kind. Congress forebodingly complied with his request and in April, 1863, enacted a law requiring of planters and farmers one-tenth of all produce of the current year. At the same time an ad valorem tax of 8 per cent was laid on farm produce held from the 1862 season; a tax of 10 per cent was placed on profits made during 1862 from the purchase and resale of almost all kinds of goods; occupational licenses were adopted, ranging from $50 to $500; and a graduated income tax was established, with rates from 1 per cent on salaries over $1,000 to 15 per cent on incomes of more than $10,000 from sources other than salary. These were heroic measures; the Charleston *Mercury* gave the tax in kind its benediction. But this tax would ultimately become as offensive to the Southern farmers as conscription.

Shadow of Defeat

Memminger and the Congress strove in vain against inflation. The funding act brought in only a negligible fraction of the outstanding notes, and by September more than $600,000,000 in paper was in circulation. Government and private citizens alike were caught in the morass of unsound finance.

The swift-rising spiral of prices brought hoarding and speculation among producers, merchants, and men with capital; it brought deprivation and bitterness among consumers and those without the means to profit from it. By late 1862 it was impossible to know one day what the price of food and clothing would be next. Temptations of profiteering were too strong for the flesh to bear; innumerable Southerners ignored the strictures of press and public, the exhortations of the government, and the pangs of conscience and yielded themselves to the seduction of easy gain. Entrepreneurs bought up and hoarded all available sugar, corn, salt, meat, molasses, whiskey, and other commodities, and manufacturers and farmers refused to sell their wares in the expectation of better prices tomorrow. Resentment among the less-favored classes waxed ominously, with groups of women in some instances staging "bread riots" in protest against runaway prices. Davis personally helped in April, 1863, to disperse a mob of angry women who were looting the stores of Richmond. To the victims of uncontrolled inflation the war was becoming an instrument for enriching the rich and impoverishing the poor.

Inflation brought other problems in its wake. Confederate commissary officers found it increasingly difficult to purchase food as government-fixed prices dropped far below those in the open market. Agents then resorted to impressment, seizing what they needed and giving certificates of indebtedness instead of money. This was often done with insolence and sometimes with brutality; it unfailingly provoked bitterness in the hearts of the victims. The evil was compounded by the contentiousness of Commissary General Lucius B. Northrop, who soon became one of the most despised men in the Confederacy. The newspapers and the people demanded relief from impressment, and Representative Foote denounced the system on the floor of Congress. In March, 1863, the Congress responded with a law requiring that price schedules be regularly published and arbitration boards set up to decide the just price of goods to be impressed. The remedy proved inadequate, and impressment took its place along with conscription and the tax in kind as a major depressant upon the spirit of the South.

If in her hour of triumph the South was sorely vexed, in the hour of defeat she was desolate. Simultaneous disasters at Gettysburg and Vicksburg cast an ominous shadow across the land, filling the steadfast with foreboding and the timid with panic. Southerners of all classes and conditions sensed the portent of these reverses. Soldiers and their families exchanged letters admitting that the war was lost. A plantation girl who knew of Vicksburg but not of Gettysburg wrote in despair, "How has the mighty fallen. . . . Our only hope is in Lee the Invincible." A Louisiana sugar planter solemnly predicted: "The end of the Confederacy is in sight." Dispirited laborers on the streets of Richmond said that they had had enough of a hopeless conflict. Robert G. H. Kean, head of the Confederate Bureau of War, wrote in his diary that the South was almost exhausted; and again, as if in prayer, "Oh, for a man at the helm like William of Orange, a man of . . . heroic character and genius, . . . a man fertile in resources, equal to emergencies."

The man at the helm, Jefferson Davis, in fact possessed many elements of heroic character, and some of genius. American history records no more unshakable devotion to a cause than that of Davis to the Confederacy. His accomplishments with inferior resources and in the face of unparalleled adversity were worthy of esteem. The British statesman William Evarts Gladstone said in the fall of 1862 that Davis had created a nation; Northern editors admitted grudgingly that he had wrought prodigies out of the material at hand, though to an evil purpose. Few men have shown more steadfast personal courage and dignity than did Davis in the hour of catastrophe. Nevertheless, he made costly mistakes. It is questionable that the Confederacy would have triumphed had these errors been avoided; failure to avoid them made defeat certain.

Ironically, one of Davis' most grievous mistakes was in the field of his deepest vanity—military affairs. He failed to give the Confederacy a unified command or a national strategy worthy of the national army which he fashioned with foresight and resourcefulness. Only through the timely concentration of a preponderance of her troops against exposed fractions of the enemy could the Confederacy hope to win. This principle was never fully applied. After Chancellorsville, Lee ought to have been appointed Confederate general in chief. Instead, Davis continued to perform this function. The nearest thing the Confederacy ever had to a unified command was three separate commands: Virginia under Lee; the Western Department under Joseph E. Johnston; and, after the fall of Vicksburg, the virtually autonomous Trans-Mississippi Department under Kirby Smith. There was deplorably little co-ordination or blending of forces among these divisions; the right hand knew not what the left hand was about.

Whether Lee would have produced a comprehensive strategy

for the South if given the opportunity is open to speculation. He commanded the Army of Northern Virginia superbly and kindled unbounded confidence in his prowess among the Southern people. One may reasonably believe that he would have risen to a broader responsibility, as did Grant in the Union cause, and would have given to the entire Confederacy the rare strategic insight and inspiring leadership that were lavished upon the more restricted theater of operations in Virginia. Such was not to be; Lee remained a mere army commander until disaster was unavoidable.

Davis' personality was ill-suited to the role he was called upon to play. Completely dedicated to the mission of defeating the enemy and establishing Southern independence, he tended to regard as a personal affront any criticism or disagreement with his methods. In this respect he resembled Woodrow Wilson of a later era; Davis found it impossible to compromise a principle, and he increasingly came to identify his own opinion with principle.

Davis is entitled to a generous measure of charity for this shortcoming; few men have ever been more severely provoked to indulge it. Beset by a powerful and relentless foe from without and fettered by the practitioners of state rights from within, he would have been more than mortal had he kept an enduring serenity. Instead, he became brittle and captious, jealously guarding the most minute prerogatives of his position and at times quarreling capriciously with subordinates and fellow citizens over points of military strategy, foreign and domestic policy, and official protocol. These clashes of personality have been explained as reflections of the very nature of Southern society. Planters fancied themselves as feudal lords holding absolute sway over manors and minions. This experience is said to have bred an exaggerated individualism that expressed itself in protest, first against the leaders of the United States, and after secession against the authorities of the Confederacy. The "bitter pride" of slavery had sown seeds of discord among the statesmen and soldiers of the South. Whatever the explanation, this vendetta of egos within the councils of the Southern republic unquestionably reduced her military potency and contributed to her destruction.

Early in the war Davis quarreled with some of the most outstanding generals of the Confederacy. This is not surprising, in view of Davis' temperament and background and the high estimate he placed on his own military insight. His keenest ambition was to lead armies in battle. Once when the Federal columns pressed close upon the South and Davis was in deep anxiety he said, "If I could take one wing and Lee the other, I think we could together wrest a victory from those people." Years after the war when asked by his daughter what he would most like to be if he could live his life over again, he replied, "I would be a cavalry officer and break squares." If without comparable experience or ambition, Lincoln often meddled for better or for worse in the plans of his generals, it is understandable that Davis should do so. But Davis dealt with men whose background and temperament were dangerously similar to his own. They were fully as jealous of their prerogatives and fully as capable of the tedious dialectics and caustic retorts to defend them. Verbal fire between the Chief Executive and his captains often waxed as hot as musketry in the field.

The most notorious of these feuds was between Davis and Joseph E. Johnston. Johnston was an aristocratic Virginian, sensitive of status, and not disposed to defer to the President's counsel on matters of strategy. Ill will first arose between them over the question of Johnston's rank in the Confederate army. He felt entitled to the top rank since he had held a higher position in the United States army than any other Confederate. Upon learning that he had been placed fourth in the order of Southern generals he sent an indignant and intemperately worded letter of protest to Davis. It accomplished nothing. Davis replied stonily, "[Your] language is, as you say, unusual; [your] arguments and statements utterly one-sided, and [your] insinuations as unfounded as they are unbecoming." Johnston remained fourth in rank and never forgot the rebuff.

Davis was displeased with Johnston's conduct of the defense of Richmond and curt phrases were exchanged. When Johnston was wounded in the battle of Seven Pines, he was replaced by Lee and never reinstated to the command of the Virginia army. Seddon persuaded Davis to assign Johnston to the Western Department, where his behavior only increased the President's disfavor. Davis and Johnston each insisted that the other misunderstood the nature and difficulties of the command. Davis held Johnston responsible and reprimanded him severely for the loss of Vicksburg; Johnston defended himself testily and demanded a court of inquiry, which was never convened. The bitterness of the long controversy between the President and the General radiated to surrounding circles of friends and supporters inside and outside the government. Senator Wigfall was an admirer of Johnston and the leader of a group of congressmen who sought to keep him in high command and clear him of all imputations of weakness or misjudgment. Richmond society was caught up in the quarrel. Mrs. Johnston and Mrs. Wigfall drew apart from Mrs. Davis; and Mary Boykin Chesnut spoke of this hostility as the "woman's war at the Spotswood [Hotel]."

Shadow of Defeat

Hostility between Davis and General Beauregard also appeared early in the war. Beauregard was a son of the high-strung Louisiana Creole aristocracy. He yearned for the role of Napoleon, and he was capable of brilliant flashes of strategic insight and combat leadership; as the hero of Fort Sumter and First Manassas, he became the *"beau sabreur, beau frappeur"* of the Confederacy. But he was often erratic and visionary, particularly in his estimates of Southern logistical capabilities. Davis and Beauregard each in effect accused the other of preventing the pursuit and destruction of the Union army after First Manassas. When presently Beauregard was assigned to the Western Department as a subordinate of Albert Sidney Johnston a friend said, "The doom is upon him." Elevated to the command of the western army upon the death of Johnston at Shiloh, Beauregard was unjustly accused of breaking off the battle at the moment of Confederate victory. He retreated before the vastly more powerful Federal army from Corinth to Tupelo, Mississippi, then left his troops in order to visit an Alabama resort for his health. Davis was furious at this unauthorized departure and peremptorily removed Beauregard from command.

Later Beauregard was assigned to command the defense of Charleston. But the friction between Davis and the Creole endured. Beauregard never forgave Davis for removing him from command of the western army, and Davis forever believed that Beauregard had squandered at Shiloh the South's greatest opportunity to destroy a major Federal force.

Animosity between Davis and Brigadier General Robert Toombs may have struck deeper into the morale of the South than the friction with Joseph E. Johnston and Beauregard. For Toombs was not only a general; he was one of the South's highest political figures as well. Toombs left the cabinet in July, 1861, in search of glory on the battlefield. He found some glory there, for he was a fearless and resourceful man. He was, however, officious and disrespectful toward his superiors and was obsessed with the favoritism that he fancied shown to West Point officers in the Confederacy. Upon failing to receive a promotion to a major generalcy when he thought his conduct at Second Manassas and Sharpsburg entitled him to it, Toombs resigned his commission in a rage. His hatred and contempt for Davis thereafter were matched only by his devotion to Southern independence. But his was a tortured devotion that entailed no loyalty to the existing government. Toombs denounced the administration without restraint, saying that independence would be gained in spite of and not because of Davis' leadership. Confederate financial policy was bitterly assailed in the newspapers by Toombs, and he joined Governor Brown of Georgia in supporting state laws to obstruct conscription and impressment. Addressing the Georgia legislature on this subject, Toombs declared impressment to be unconstitutional and tyrannical. He later took a commission in the Georgia state forces, where he carried on a career of vituperation and obstruction that at times bordered on mutiny. It possibly would have been astute to humor Toombs with a promotion in the Confederate army, for his alienation wreaked incalculable harm upon the Southern cause. Professor Frank Owsley has truly said, "The Confederacy was really not big enough for both Toombs and Davis. . . ."

If the President's disfavor for certain of his generals withered Southern morale, so did his dogged loyalty for others. This trait first appeared in his refusal to bow to public demand and remove Albert Sidney Johnston after the loss of Forts Henry and Donelson. In Johnston's case Davis' judgment was later vindicated; in others it was not. This unpopular constancy is best observed in his support of Commissary General Lucius Northrop and General Braxton Bragg.

Northrop was a favorite mark for Confederate censure. A more difficult and thankless task than feeding the Southern army with the available supplies, money, and transportation would be hard to imagine; Northrop may have done as well as possible under the circumstances, though he unquestionably was an indiscreet and contentious man. The people of the South thought him also incompetent. One would be pressed to find a single favorable comment about Northrop, except in the writings of Davis and the President's staunchest supporter among Confederate scribes, Mary Boykin Chesnut. Mrs. Chesnut wrote disdainfully in 1861: "If I were to pick out the best-abused man in Richmond . . . I should say Mr. Commissary General Northrop was the most cursed and vilified. He is held accountable for everything that goes wrong in the army." Confederate commanders were unanimously critical of the Commissary General; the patient Lee once lectured Northrop sternly on the responsibilities of his department. Joseph E. Johnston and Beauregard considered him unfit. The press railed against Northrop, and Representative Foote once assaulted him bodily in a committee meeting. Davis was unmoved. He and Northrop had been friends before the war, and the President defended the unpopular officer and kept him at his post almost to the end, contrary to the wishes of the entire Confederacy.

Bragg was the most controversial of Southern generals, and the most discredited. History has been severe to Bragg. He was a man of sterling devotion to the Confederate cause and an officer of extraordinary talent in certain aspects of his calling.

As an organizer, instructor, and disciplinarian of troops he was without peer; and the Confederate army had sore need of these skills. Bragg's were the best-drilled soldiers at Shiloh, where, as Albert Sidney Johnston's chief of staff, he did yeoman service in readying the entire Southern force for its first great trial by fire. Assigned later to command the western army, Bragg showed by his campaign into Kentucky in the fall 1862 that he was capable of bold and imaginative strategy.

Yet Bragg's shortcomings outweighed his assets as an independent commander. He was obstinate and fault-finding with subordinates. A sense of discipline perhaps suitable for regular troops was too demanding for volunteers and conscripts; Bragg was said once to have had a man executed for killing a chicken while on the march. Above all, Bragg lacked the spark of leadership to kindle full confidence among his soldiers and the stern volition to drive home a victory. Opposition to Bragg first became serious as a result of the faltering and unsuccessful Kentucky campaign; a storm of protest broke against him after the battle of Murfreesboro. His corps commanders said explicitly that they preferred another chief, and the newspapers of the South were unremitting in their censure. Davis confirmed his faith in Bragg, but directed the commander of the Western Department, Joseph E. Johnston, to investigate and relieve Bragg if he felt it advisable. Johnston made the investigation, but shrank from grasping the baton. Bragg was left in command, a source of increasing contention between Davis and Congress and between Davis and the South.

Defeat in the field and distress around the hearthstones of the South sharpened the asperity between Davis and the congressional opposition. Wigfall in the Senate and Foote in the House remorselessly scored every measure of the administration for the prosecution of the war. The views of these men were irreconcilable, except for a common hatred of Davis and his cabinet and supporters. Wigfall approved the major policies of the government, such as conscription, impressment, and the tax in kind, but claimed that the war was being lost through the incompetent administration of them. This belief was shared by Senator William L. Yancey. Wigfall was a man of massive frame and tigerish eyes who voiced his disdain of Davis in baleful flashes of invective. Foote opposed the policies themselves, and, if possible, hated Davis even more intensely than did Wigfall. Foote was small and bald and of "colicky delivery," but an implacable antagonist. Together, Wigfall and Foote incalculably weakened the Southern cause.

During the first two years of the war the administration was generally supported by a majority in Congress and was able to carry most of its measures in spite of determined opposition. But Gettysburg and Vicksburg took their toll among Davis' supporters when congressional elections were held in the fall of 1863. The President was too preoccupied with military affairs to lend assistance to his adherents, and the popular mood was such as to have rendered it futile if he had. Many co-operative congressmen were defeated at the polls, and numerous others who had upheld the Davis government earlier in the war now joined the opposition. By 1864 every representative from the state of South Carolina was hostile to Davis; and thus it went throughout the South. The Confederacy entered her greatest trial with Congress and the Chief Executive hopelessly split.

VII

Failure of King Cotton Diplomacy

Confederate statesmen turned to Europe for diplomatic recognition and assistance in the struggle against the North. In doing so, they were mindful of the French alliance that had been essential to the success of the American Revolution. If England and France could be induced to aid the Confederacy, she would be assured of survival; otherwise, her future was uncertain. Upon diplomacy as upon domestic statesmanship and military strategy hung the destiny of the Southern republic.

In foreign affairs above all, the South relied upon the preeminence of King Cotton. This imperious sovereign would be admitted instantly to the council chambers, treasuries, and arsenals of Europe, thought the people of the Confederacy. The foremost authority on Confederate diplomacy has called this the greatest example of the willingness of the Old South to risk its life on an idea.

There was a certain logic behind this faith. For years the Southern people had heard from the lips of Englishmen and

Failure of King Cotton Diplomacy

Americans that the economy of England depended completely upon cotton, and that the economies of New England and France were almost as dependent upon the white fiber. Without cotton, it was said, the great textile industries of Europe and America would languish and their prosperity wither. The nations of Europe could not permit the Confederacy to be blockaded and destroyed. They would be forced by the threat of a cotton famine to extend diplomatic recognition and succor in money and arms; and if necessary, they must intervene in the American conflict in order to preserve the source of their wealth. Traveling through the South in 1861, William Howard Russell of the London *Times* heard this on every tongue. England was considered by Southerners a mere appanage of the Cotton Kingdom, he declared. "Why sir," said a South Carolinian voicing the general opinion, "we have only to shut off your supply of cotton for a few weeks and we can create a revolution in Great Britain. There are four millions of your people depending on us for their bread, not to speak of the many millions of dollars. No, sir, we know that England must recognize us." This conviction was held by the leaders as well as the common folk of the South. Governors of states and members of Congress freely proclaimed it. Davis and his cabinet believed it and made it the heart of their foreign policy.

The Southern people were led by this overweening confidence in the power of cotton to a dangerous complacency toward the nations that were their potential allies. Southerners took for granted the certainty of recognition and adopted a strategy of coercion rather than of persuasion in seeking it; they would force the hands of England and France by withholding cotton from their looms. In the summer and fall of 1861, Southern spokesmen began to urge an embargo on cotton.

The Confederacy

Planters and shippers were besought to hold back their produce in order to make the Europeans more keenly aware of their dependence upon the South. For reasons of diplomacy the Confederate government shunned an official embargo, but encouraged a voluntary one. The response of the Southern people was almost complete; the cotton remained at home. Though the 1861 harvest was one of the heaviest in the annals of the crop, virtually none of it reached the ports of Europe. A perceptive student of this epoch has written, "No embargo in history has been any more strict." King Cotton diplomacy was about to be put to the supreme test.

In the spring of 1861 Davis appointed three emissaries to represent the Confederacy in the capitals of Europe. They were William L. Yancey of Alabama, Judge Pierre Rost of Louisiana, and A. Dudley Mann of Georgia. Measured by the gravity and delicacy of their task, these men were ill-chosen. Only Yancey was highly distinguished, and he was not a diplomat. He was the foremost orator of the Old South, without peer in exhorting his people to secession, but hardly the man for the subtleties of European statecraft. Mrs. Mary Boykin Chesnut disparaged him in her famous diary as being offensive to the English because he had killed his father-in-law in a street brawl. Far more objectionable was his vehement advocacy of slavery, an institution universally abhorred in England. The Southerners who accompanied Yancey were respected citizens, but without distinction in affairs of state. The men did not fit the mission.

Instructions of Provisional Secretary of State Robert Toombs to the Confederate emissaries were designed to appeal to the British sense of legal propriety as well as their concern for material well-being. Secession was to be presented, not as revolution, but as the exercise of a constitutional right whose present justification sprang from the oppression of the South by the majority North. Legal, moral, and material aspects of the Southern case were to be astutely blended; the protective tariff exacting tribute of the South was to be given as the supreme example of Northern oppression. This, thought Toombs, would stir the sympathy of the free-trading English, whose commerce was cramped by the tariff. The crowning argument was to be made on the role of cotton in the world economy, with a "delicate allusion" to the dependence of English prosperity upon the Southern staple and the disastrous consequences to be expected of prolonged hostilities between North and South.

Hope of early diplomatic recognition was vain. A heavy surplus of cotton lay in British warehouses; and the Confederacy had done nothing to prove her ability to endure as a nation. On May 3 British Foreign Minister Lord John Russell received the Confederate emissaries in discreet silence, heard their case, and made no commitment.

Early in May, in response to President Lincoln's proclamation of the Federal blockade of Southern ports, Queen Victoria's government issued a statement of neutrality recognizing the Confederacy as a belligerent power. This development came as a windfall to the South, and not as the harvest of diplomacy. It was expedient to British economy, for it permitted her merchants to sell to North and South alike, free of the responsibility of aiding rebellion. France quickly followed suit. Gaining belligerent status was a great advantage to the Confederacy, since it gave her access to the markets of England and France. It also inspired the hope of future diplomatic success. But it was far short of recognition as an independent nation, and even more remote from military assistance or alliance. Yancey presently returned to enter the Southern Senate; Rost moved on to Spain, and Mann to Belgium. The challenge to Confederate diplomacy remained unmastered.

As these emissaries sought recognition and aid of the major European states, the Confederate government endeavored to cultivate friendship among the nations on her own borders. This required tact, for the ante-bellum South had traditionally coveted their territory. Charles Helm of Kentucky was dispatched to Havana where he directed shipping through the Federal blockade. Helm explained the earlier Southern ambition to annex Cuba as having grown out of the necessity of a political balance against the North in the United States Senate. An independent Confederacy would feel no such need, he assured the Cuban authorities.

The Confederate emissary to the Juárez government of Mexico was John T. Pickett of Kentucky, former United States consul at Vera Cruz. A more unfortunate choice was scarcely possible. Pickett was an intemperate and belligerent man. Worst of all, he was a filibusterer, who earlier had plotted the annexation of Mexico to the United States and whose contempt for Mexican culture was only thinly disguised. Pickett bluntly advocated seeking recognition through bribery, with "a million or so judiciously applied." Totally wanting in discretion, Pickett sometimes insulted Mexican honor without being aware of his gaucheries. On one occasion he was jailed for assaulting an American citizen in Mexico City. Understandably, his blundering efforts to gain recognition failed, and ultimately he was recalled by the Confederate government.

Though unsuccessful in negotiating with the national government of Mexico, the Confederacy was able during most of the war to carry on a vital commerce in arms and supplies through the Mexican port of Matamoros. This was possible because of near-anarchy in Mexico which left many of the border states virtually independent. To the state of Nuevo León, Davis in May, 1861, sent one of the most resourceful of all Confederate agents, Juan A. Quintero. Quintero was a native of Cuba and a citizen of Texas. With great diplomatic skill he persuaded the Mexican authorities in control of Matamoros (including, later in the war, Juárez and the Emperor Maximilian) to leave open this line of Confederate supply.

In the fall of 1861, Davis appointed a new diplomatic mission to Europe to attempt what the first had failed to accomplish. James M. Mason of Virginia was sent to England, and John Slidell of Louisiana to France. These selections were not ideal, but the two men possessed public experience and ability. They were more suitable than their predecessors. Mason was an aristocratic planter-politician, a former United States Senator, and the grandson of George Mason, author of the Virginia Declaration of Rights. Though the Confederate emissary was accused of provincialism in speech and manners—particularly of a careless spray of tobacco juice—he was a man of warmth and intelligence. His gravest handicap as representative to England was that he epitomized the proslavery spirit, for he was the author of the ill-famed fugitive slave act of 1850. Slidell was famous as an astute politician. He had been an outstanding figure in the Democratic party in the 1850's and, like Mason, was a former United States Senator; he spoke French acceptably and was married to a daughter of the Louisiana Creole aristocracy. The South expected and the North feared great results of Slidell.

The most dramatic episode in the diplomatic careers of

The Confederacy

Mason and Slidell occurred before they reached their destinations. On November 8 they were seized aboard the British ship "Trent" by Captain Charles Wilkes of the Union navy and placed behind bars. The North was jubilant; but England resented the trespass upon her vessel and demanded release of the two Confederates. Lincoln and his cabinet set them free. This was a wise decision, for testy British Prime Minister Lord Palmerston was in a belligerent mood. It is high irony that the Confederate diplomats probably came nearer to achieving the one thing that could have assured Southern independence—that is, foreign intervention—while in a Boston prison than later over the conference table.

Toombs was now gone from the Southern cabinet, and former United States Senator Robert M. T. Hunter of Virginia was Secretary of State. Hunter adopted the main features of his predecessor's policy and set them anew to catch the prevailing winds of diplomacy. Mason and Slidell were instructed to emphasize the commercial advantages that Europe could expect of an independent Confederacy. The Northern blockade was to be challenged on the ground that it was not effective and therefore violated the Declaration of Paris of 1856, which outlawed "paper" blockades. Diplomatic recognition was to be requested on the premise that Southern independence was inevitable, but that it would be hastened by the moral support of foreign acknowledgment, thus shortening the duration of useless bloodshed. Neither European alliance nor intervention was explicitly sought at this time.

The two emissaries arrived in Europe in January, 1862. The moment seemed auspicious for Confederate diplomacy. The Northern army was halted in its tracks; and, whereas the first overseas mission from the South had reached the capitals of Europe before the cotton embargo was undertaken, Mason and Slidell came at the height of it. British reserves of fiber were fast dwindling, and mill owners and laborers alike looked anxiously toward the future. France faced a similar plight.

British sentiment toward the American Civil War was mixed. The ruling classes generally favored the Confederacy. Landed aristocrats looked more kindly upon the plantation society of the South than upon the commercial and laboring community of the North, and many English industrialists and shippers welcomed the prospect of a great Southern market free of prohibitive tariffs. Both groups yearned for a brake upon the rising strength of a united America, for they knew that a multiplicity of nations beyond the Atlantic would be less of a rival and threat to England than a single colossus. An editor stated the case:

We do not see why three or four independent republics . . . will not answer better than one absorbing and overwhelming dominion. We are certain that such an arrangement will be more conducive to the civilization of America. Limitation will produce modesty and caution. . . . There may be jealousies and quarrels—as there are among contiguous European countries; but we are much inclined to think that these, even if they occasionally proceed to bloodshed, will have a far less demoralizing influence on all concerned than the conviction of boundless power and unmatched grandeur which now inflates the bosom, disturbs the brain and damages the principles and sense of justice of nearly every American citizen. The several commonwealths will keep each other in order. . . .

A significant faction in Parliament supported the South. Leaders of this group were William S. Lindsay, John A. Roebuck, W. H. Gregory, and Alexander James Beresford Beresford-

Hope. Many English writers and intellectuals favored the Confederacy, including Thomas Carlyle, Charles Darwin, and Lord Tennyson.

On the other hand, British laboring classes sympathized with the North because they felt that she was fighting for democracy. For the same reason, liberal reformers such as John Bright, Richard Cobden, and W. E. Forster upheld the Union cause. Slavery was condemned by all classes in England, including Confederate supporters, who at first did not believe that emancipation was one of the aims of the Lincoln government in waging the war.

The British public provided fertile soil for Confederate propaganda, and large sections of the press welcomed it. The London *Times*, greatest of English newspapers, was in sympathy with the South, as was the *Manchester Guardian*, chief spokesman of the industrial north country. Many other newspapers were of like persuasion, and they opened their columns to Southern views on secession and Southern accounts from the battlefield. One of the most influential of British propagandists was James Spence, a hired Confederate agent. In 1862 Spence published a book called *The American Union* that was a blend of American history and Southern polemic. It upheld the constitutionality of secession and emphasized the superiority of Southern culture over that of the North. Spence concluded that England as well as the South would be blessed by a division of the American republic.

Master propagandist of the Confederacy was Henry Hotze. Hotze was a native of Switzerland who had migrated to America before the war and had served on the staff of the Mobile *Register*. In the fall of 1862 he was commissioned by Secretary of State Hunter to lay the case of the Confederacy before the people of Europe. Hotze arrived in London with little money, but with winning ways, a keen mind, and an unerring editorial instinct. He quickly gained the confidence of the leading editors of England, and presently was contributing articles on the war to the newspapers of both of the English political parties. In May, 1862, Hotze established in London the *Index*, a journal of news and comment on the Confederacy and the war. Hotze invited and received columns on the war from the ablest journalists of England, thus astutely converting these men into Confederate propagandists when they wrote for English newspapers. The *Index* was held in high repute, for its tone was one of poise and dignity, and not of vituperation. Hotze brilliantly expounded the Southern view of secession, the military campaigns, and the blockade; he worked mightily to dissuade European men, especially the Irish, from migrating to America to swell the Union armies; and he studied British public opinion with a sure eye and passed his judgments on to the Secretary of State and to Mason. Late in the war he extended his activities to France with equal success. Possibly no other man accomplished as much for the Southern cause overseas as did Henry Hotze.

Napoleon III of France had a more pressing and tangible reason for supporting the Confederacy than did England; he coveted Mexico. He feared to seize his prey as long as the United States was one nation; but war between North and South gave him an opportunity to strike with safety, and he felt that a permanent division of the American republic would assure French hegemony over the neighboring country. Napoleon yearned for Confederate victory, and the reports of French Minister Count Henri Mercier from the United States stirred the hope of its fulfilment. But the Emperor was uneasy over affairs in Europe, where he could become involved in war at any moment. The French army and navy must not be trapped in faraway America with a hostile British fleet commanding the Atlantic. Only with England's assent would Napoleon dare invade Mexico, and only with England as an ally would he recognize the Confederacy and embroil himself in the American conflict. Thus England held the key to Southern diplomatic hopes.

Both Mason and Slidell were cordially received in the countries to which they were accredited. Mason was favored with the hospitality of many of the leading figures of England, and especially those merchants, shipowners, and members of Parliament who supported the Confederacy. These men instructed the Southern envoy regarding the tone of British public opinion and guided him in his overtures to the government. Slidell was welcomed into the highest circles of French society and repeatedly given audience with Foreign Minister Thouvenel and with the Emperor himself.

In early February, 1862, Slidell talked with Foreign Minister Thouvenel of France and Mason conferred with Lord Russell. The European statesmen were courteous but stonily reserved. Slidell urged that the blockade was illegal because it was ineffective; that four hundred ships had run it during the first four months of its operation. Thouvenel countered with the embarrassing question: Why does not more cotton reach France if the blockade is impotent? The Confederate emissary was evasive, for he must not acknowledge that the cotton shortage was the result of a self-imposed embargo. Presently the Emperor and the French Senate made clear the intention of France for the moment to remain neutral. Napoleon found no choice but to acquiesce in the Federal blockade as long as England did so.

Early in March, 1862, Southern sympathizers in the British Parliament sought to force the government to take action against the blockade. Led by Gregory, they opened debate challenging the effectiveness and legality of the blockade and presenting Mason's statistics on the number of ships that had passed through it. The attempt was ill-timed; Northern victories at Roanoke Island and Forts Henry and Donelson had dimmed the prospect of Confederate success. John Bright and W. E. Forster replied convincingly to the pro-Confederate spokesmen and asked the same question that Thouvenel had asked Slidell: Why the scarcity and expensiveness of cotton in England if the blockade was a fiction? Gregory and his associates had no ready answer. Foreign Minister Lord Russell held the blockade to be a real one, and the move in Parliament for British intervention died in the bud.

In March Judah P. Benjamin became Confederate Secretary of State, a position which he would hold until the end of the war. Affairs of battlefield and home front now claimed virtually all of Davis' energies. He held frequent council with his friend and confidant, Benjamin, who kept him informed on developments overseas, but the new Secretary was given free rein in the management of them. Benjamin discharged his duties with ability and came to be called by some "the brains of the Confederacy." Yet he inaugurated no sweeping change in Southern diplomatic policy; cotton continued to lie at the root of it. Benjamin instructed the Confederate envoys anew to challenge the legality of the blockade on the ground of ineffectiveness, and he supported this point with additional statistics on the number of violations. His argument for diplomatic recognition was more subtle than heretofore; recognition would end the war, he said, for it would present the Northern government with an impartial verdict concerning the permanency of the Confederacy. Benjamin played his hand with alertness and ingenuity, but his opponents held most of the high cards.

By early spring the cotton shortage was beginning to pinch the French textile industry, and Napoleon's government looked fearfully upon the prospect of social and political unrest among the millworkers. Again the Emperor considered intervention, and Thouvenel authorized Minister Mercier to sound out Seward on the possibility of mediation by France. But portents from the battlefield were not favorable to this end. Union diplomacy was stiffened by military success, and when Mercier approached Seward to complain of French economic distress and suggest mediation, the American statesman delivered a bold riposte. He rebuked France for having recognized Confederate belligerency, saying that this alone had kept the war alive. The quickest way for France to get cotton, Seward declared, was to extinguish this source of Southern hope.

All forces in Europe interested in Southern victory—Confederate diplomats, English supporters of the South, and Napoleon—now redoubled their efforts to bring about joint mediation or intervention by England and France. Member of Parliament W. S. Lindsay sailed to France in April and discussed the matter personally with the Emperor. Napoleon assured the British interventionist that he was anxious to join England in a move to end the American war. Nevertheless, the affair came to naught. Palmerston and Russell refused to acknowledge this under-the-table diplomacy and denied Lindsay an opportunity to present his message from across the Channel. For the time being, British leaders preferred to regard the American conflict from afar.

The diplomatic stroke of the Confederacy was thus caught at dead center. European intervention would probably assure the South of success; the French government earnestly desired to intervene but feared to do so without the co-operation of Great Britain; and the British government balked at positive action until the course of the war should become distinct. Benjamin determined to break the impasse by a new appeal to Napoleon for French intervention alone, for the Confederate statesman felt that if France could be induced to take the step, England would certainly follow. On April 12, Benjamin sent Slidell additional instructions for the accomplishment of this end.

Slidell was to offer the Emperor a highly tempting commercial convention and an outright bribe in return for the breaking of the Federal blockade. France was to be granted free trade with the Confederacy "for a certain defined period," the precise length of time to be at Slidell's discretion. Since the Emperor's finances were under "temporary embarrassment," Slidell was, if necessary, to offer him 100,000 bales of cotton to meet the cost of sending the French navy to break the blockade. Both nations would prosper from the commerce that would follow, said the Secretary of State. French vessels would arrive at Confederate ports in convoy, laden with arms and munitions and the other necessities of the South, and would return to France with cotton for her hungry mills. Perhaps as much as one million bales would be exchanged in this traffic. Slidell might make the same offer in return for diplomatic recognition instead of naval intervention, if he thought it more feasible.

Either would bring about Southern independence, thought Benjamin: "If the [breaking of the blockade] would enable us to drive the invaders from our soil by force of arms, [recognition] would by its moral effect produce an earlier peace. . . . There is every reason to believe that our recognition would be the signal for the immediate organization of a large and influential party in the Northern States favorable to putting an end to the war." A week later the Confederate Congress authorized Davis to make treaties with Great Britain, France, and Spain granting trade concessions and other privileges in return for intervention. King Cotton had become a diplomatic realist.

Benjamin's offer reached Slidell in July, 1862, along with news of Confederate victories in the Shenandoah Valley and on the Virginia Peninsula. The moment had arrived, thought the Southern commissioner, for the supreme effort to induce Napoleon to come to the assistance of the South. An opportunity for this was presently forthcoming when Slidell was invited to a personal interview with the Emperor.

The meeting took place at Vichy. Napoleon freely expressed his admiration and sympathy for the Confederacy and his desire to intervene, along with England, in behalf of the South. Slidell replied with an astute argument favoring intervention. He again attacked the Northern blockade as a violation of the Declaration of Paris, and implored Napoleon to repudiate it in order that French ships might bear arms and supplies to the beleaguered South. Seward's threat of war was a bluff, Slidell declared, for a single French ironclad could destroy the blockade. A victorious North would never agree to a French regime in Mexico, Slidell truly argued, hence it would behoove France to throw her weight against the common enemy. Finally, Benjamin's cotton bait was artfully exposed; the Emperor would receive not less than 100,000, and perhaps as much as 500,000, bales of fiber in return for breaking the blockade. Napoleon made no promises, but he was clearly interested. Slidell left the interview in high spirit.

Southern emissaries now for the first time presented formal requests for recognition to the governments of France and England. But the notes met with no success. Russell refused an interview with Mason and on August 2 replied unfavorably to the demand for recognition; the time had not yet arrived for such a step, he said. Slidell's note was more cordially received by Napoleon's government, but Thouvenel let the Southern commissioner know that the Emperor could take no positive action at the moment. Though Slidell probably anticipated this, he grew despondent over Confederate diplomatic prospects. He now began presciently to suspect that England was complacent over the duration of the war, as long as she continued to prosper and her American rival to suffer from it. This melancholy was dispelled in September by news of Lee's great victory at Second Manassas and by rumors that the British government was about to consider some form of intervention to end the war.

These rumors had substance. The aloofness of Palmerston and Russell toward Mason was deceptive. By fall 1862 the British statesmen were increasingly concerned over the shrinking reserves of cotton as well as being impressed by Confederate military prowess. Unknown either to Mason or to United States Minister Charles Francis Adams, the two British leaders, along with Chancellor of the Exchequer Gladstone, were planning ways for bringing the war in America to a close. As the news of Lee's march into Maryland reached Europe, the British leaders came to a decision. If the Confederates should win another great victory or take a major Northern city, such as Washington or Baltimore, then an overture was to be made to both warring parties that they cease fighting and come to terms of separation, with England and France serving as mediators, along with Russia if she could be induced to do so. If the North should reject the offer but the South accept it, then the independence of the South would be recognized. Should in the forthcoming test of arms the advantage fall to the North, said Palmerston, "We may wait awhile and see what may follow. . . ."

The enthusiasm of Russell and Gladstone in favor of recognizing the Confederacy outdistanced that of Palmerston. They feared the impending cotton famine and unrest among the millworkers more than the wrath of the United States. As late as October 7, Gladstone declared at Newcastle that Jefferson Davis had made an army and a nation and that the separation of the South from the North was permanent. Russell presently repeated these opinions in a note to the British cabinet recommending an armistice in America to pave the way for negotiating terms of separation.

Meantime, Napoleon pressed for joint recognition and intervention with all the means at his disposal. He was guided in his thinking by his own instincts and by the advice of Minister Mercier. Mercier had the preceding April been permitted by Seward to visit Richmond to determine firsthand the depth of Southern resistance. Seward doubtless believed that Mercier would be struck by the weakness of the Confederacy; instead, after talking at length with Benjamin and other Southern leaders, Mercier returned to Washington convinced of the impossibility of imposing Federal authority upon the South. He wrote this opinion to Thouvenel at the time and repeated it after each Confederate victory during the summer. On September 30 he wrote that the time had come for France to propose mediation.

On October 26, Slidell was granted a second interview with Napoleon. The Emperor spoke with warm sympathy of the Confederacy and her fortitude, and he brought forth a specific proposal for joint action with England and Russia: an armistice of six months was to be arranged between North and South, with Southern ports open to the commerce of the world. If such a suspension of hostilities should occur, said Napoleon, the war would never be resumed and Southern independence would be made a reality. England was on the point of joining France in the overture, he said. Slidell was still doubtful of British intentions, and again he importuned the Emperor to act alone, and offered free trade, a cotton bonus, and Confederate approval of French suzerainty in Mexico as rewards. But Napoleon would not act alone. Presently he sent to the British government his formal recommendation of a joint effort to establish an armistice and lift the blockade.

Napoleon did not know that Palmerston's ardor for intervention had cooled before the French proposal was written. For the Prime Minister's words to Russell calling for a Confederate military victory held the key to Southern hopes of recognition. Only a triumph of such magnitude as to convince Palmerston that the North had been rendered harmless would have induced him to take the step. Palmerston feared the North. Seward's threats of war weighed heavily upon him; Canada and the British merchant fleet must not lightly be placed in jeopardy. Lee's reverse at Sharpsburg in mid-September destroyed the possibility of British recognition at that time. Upon receiving word of the battle, Palmerston wrote that the time was not ripe for action. "Ten days or a fortnight more may throw a light upon future prospects," he said. The Confederate army withdrew to Virginia, and on November 11 the British cabinet considered and rejected Napoleon's proposal of a joint overture for an armistice. Britain resumed her role of waiting and watching, and Napoleon restively did the same.

This was the climax of Confederate negotiations for recognition. It is conceivable that England and France would have extended recognition if Lee had won decisively at Sharpsburg, and much has been made of this possibility. Benjamin and other Confederates believed that Southern victory would have been assured by it, and historian E. D. Adams has written, "Had that plan [mediation and recognition] been adopted . . . there is little question that . . . war would have ensued between England and the North [and] . . . the independence of the South would have been established." But the consequences of recognition alone are problematical. Palmerston in fact made it clear that England ought to remain neutral even if she should acknowledge Confederate independence. Without assistance from Europe in the form of money, arms, and the breaking of the blockade, the South quite likely would have been defeated anyway. Only if the Lincoln government had insisted upon going to war over recognition would it certainly have saved the Confederacy.

Confederate diplomats had relied upon agitation among unemployed cotton mill laborers to force the British government to break the blockade in order to secure cotton. By 1863 the cotton famine was upon England and more than 400,000 mill operatives were idle. Many were on the point of starvation. Nevertheless, the mill hands generally remained sympathetic toward the Northern cause, and no uprising occurred. Abhorrence of slavery on moral grounds is usually considered the major reason for this continued sympathy for the Union. William L. Yancey sensed this attitude among the workers early in the war, and the perceptive Henry Hotze thought that they were primarily guided by it. But it seems unlikely that distaste for an institution in a distant land would cause men to permit their families to starve. Fully as strong among the laborers as their repugnance for slavery was the belief that their own future welfare was in some way bound to Union victory. They were repeatedly told this by their own political champions. John Bright said, "Not only is the question of Negro slavery concerned in this struggle, but . . . the freedom of white men is not safe in [Southern] hands." In a powerful anti-Southern book *The Slave Power*, John Cairnes warned British workers that if the Confederacy should win the war her goal then would be to spread slavery throughout the remainder of the world. Self-interest was blended with righteous anger to keep peace among the mill laborers and thwart Confederate diplomacy.

There were now other causes for Confederate alarm over diplomatic affairs in Europe. A Confederate naval fleet was being lost. Early in the war Secretary of the Navy Mallory had commissioned Captain James D. Bulloch and Lieutenant James H. North to purchase fighting craft and commerce raiders in Europe. Many raiders were acquired, and led by the famed "Alabama," they virtually destroyed the American merchant marine. In addition to the raiders, a number of powerful iron-clad rams were being constructed for the Confederacy by the Lairds of Birkenhead and other British shipbuilders. These ships were probably capable of destroying the Federal navy.

The Confederacy

By fall 1863 they would be ready to sail. Gathering abundant evidence to prove that these vessels were destined for the Confederacy, United States Minister Charles Francis Adams urged Lord Russell to seize them on the ground that their sale to a belligerent would be an unneutral act. Adams hinted that it would result in war between the United States and England. Benjamin sensed the danger and in March wrote to Mason advising that the rams be transferred to France for possible resale to the Confederacy. Early in April the raider "Alexandra" was seized. Although the vessel was released by the courts for want of proof that she was being armed for the service of a nation at war, the seizure itself indicated the growing aloofness of the British government toward the South. Ultimately, in the fall 1863, the unfinished rams were seized by Lord Russell and turned over to the British navy. Not only did Russell fear war with the United States if the rams should reach the Confederacy, but England dared not set a precedent of a neutral power building ships for a belligerent.

By spring 1863 the major Confederate venture in overseas finance was faltering badly. This was the Erlanger Loan. The prominent French banking firm of Emile Erlanger & Company had proposed to market in Europe $25,000,000 in Confederate cotton bonds—interest-bearing bonds exchangeable at a fixed low price for cotton owned by the Confederate government. Benjamin was not enthusiastic over the plan because he considered the rate of interest (8 per cent) and the profit to be made by the Erlangers to be too high. The French bankers were to receive the bonds at 30 per cent discount. Slidell urgently supported the loan, for he thought that it would influence the Emperor to recognize the Confederacy. Benjamin reluctantly approved it, but succeeded in reducing the amount of the loan to $15,000,000, the interest rate to 7 per cent, and the discount to 23 per cent. When in March the bonds were placed on the market they at first sold rapidly and at a favorable price. Soon the price began to drop alarmingly. Pressed by the Erlangers, Mason used money received from the sale of the first installment in order to purchase in the market and keep up the price of the bonds. For a few weeks this succeeded, but news of the Confederate loss of Vicksburg caused the price to plummet. Out of the entire transaction, the Confederacy retained $2,599,000 in cash and was able to use the repurchased bonds to pay off about $5,000,000 in old debts to British bankers. Purchasers of the bonds, principally British friends of the South, lost all of their investment upon the fall of the Confederacy. Napoleon was not moved by the Erlanger Loan in his attitude toward recognizing the Southern republic.

Again it was victory in the field (Chancellorsville on May 1–4, 1863) that kindled hopes of recognition among Southern diplomats and supporters. British friends of the Confederacy bestirred themselves instantly, arranging mass meetings of sympathy in the cotton textile districts and planning another stroke in Parliament to force recognition upon the reluctant cabinet. On June 18, Slidell again met with Napoleon, and again urged upon him the wisdom of French intervention alone if England failed to co-operate. Napoleon agreed in principle, but said that he could not afford the risk, and especially not at the moment, for fear of a European war with Prussia over the Polish question.

Two days later Lindsay and Roebuck arrived from England and met with Napoleon to discuss strategy for bringing the British government to join France in recognizing the Confederacy. The Emperor was wary and refused their request for another formal overture to England; he pointed out that the first one had been disclosed by Russell to the United States government, thereby causing resentment against France. The Emperor did, however, authorize the British lawmakers to deny in Parliament that he had changed his position on the question of recognition, as Palmerston now alleged.

On June 30 Roebuck placed before Parliament a formal motion for the recognition of Confederate independence. His argument was primarily addressed to British self-interest and security. A united America was fast becoming a colossus that would tyrannize the world if not split into rival nations, he warned. He then challenged the statements that Napoleon had lost interest in the Confederacy, and disclosed the substance of his interview with the Emperor, including Napoleon's accusation of perfidy on the part of the British government. Roebuck's indiscreet statements did more harm than good; even friends of the South found it necessary to oppose him under the circumstances. Palmerston remained firm against recognition, and a few days later Gettysburg and Vicksburg lent the weight of iron to his judgment.

Failure of the Roebuck proposal made clear the impossibility of inducing the Palmerston government to recognize the Confederacy. Realization of this lit the fires of resentment toward England among the leaders and people of the South. The final acts were played by Benjamin. Early in August, 1863, he wrote Mason to leave England, and the commissioner promptly joined Slidell in Paris. A month later the Secretary of State summoned the Confederate cabinet in Davis' absence and peremptorily expelled all British consuls from the South. King Cotton diplomacy was dead.

Failure of King Cotton Diplomacy

After the diplomatic "break" with England, Benjamin and Slidell continued to do everything in their power to induce Napoleon alone to intervene in behalf of the Confederacy. Their greatest hope now lay in the Mexican pawn. Assured of the support of French troops, in 1863 Maximilian of Austria assented to become Emperor of Mexico. Slidell again warned Napoleon that Northern victory would bring disaster to French plans for an empire in North America. The Emperor of France did not have to be reminded of this by Slidell. After the Union military successes of the summer of 1863, Seward made this perfectly clear. Still Napoleon could not be moved beyond expressions of sympathy for the South.

Benjamin now sought to influence the master through the puppet; he appealed to Maximilian in the hope that Maximilian could prevail upon Napoleon to aid the South. The Emperor of Mexico had already indicated a desire for France to recognize the Confederacy. In the fall of 1863, William Preston of Kentucky, former United States Minister to Spain, was appointed Confederate envoy to Mexico. But the Southern plan died in birth. In spite of his fear of the North, Napoleon now fatuously believed it possible to gain recognition of the Maximilian government by the United States. Preston never reached Mexico City. He journeyed instead to Europe to hold council with Maximilian's agents, who upon instructions from Napoleon remained aloof to all Confederate proposals.

The South's diplomatic failure was crucial; it doomed her to defeat. It is reasonable to believe that Confederate independence would have been assured by European recognition and intervention. What France and her European allies had done for the American Colonies in revolt, England and France could have done for the Confederacy. Abundant explanations are at hand for the refusal of England—and consequently of France—to support the Confederacy. These include: the ineptitude of Confederate diplomats; the moral stigma of slavery; the importation of cotton from India, Egypt, and Brazil to replace Southern fiber; the importance of Northern wheat in feeding the English population; the persistent belief among British leaders that Confederate independence would be achieved without European intervention; Northern victories in the field at critical moments early in the war, followed by the general decline of Confederate military prospects later; fear of war with the North and the possible loss of Canada and the British merchant fleet; and the immense war profits being made by English merchants and industrialists as the struggle lengthened. Doubtless many or all of these factors bore upon the British choice against intervention, for no single one appears to have been decisive. One conclusion only is certain. The Southern people and their leaders had exaggerated the power of King Cotton to bring the world to terms. British statesmen rightly judged that Southern independence was not vital to British security or prosperity, and the Confederacy was left to her own resources and to her fate.

VIII

A Divided South and Total War

Autumn of 1863 brought no relief from a summer of travail. On September 19–20 Bragg struck and defeated the Union army under Rosecrans in the great battle of Chickamauga near Chattanooga, then Bragg faltered and wasted the golden opportunity for the kill. His subordinate commanders were stirred to the point of mutiny by this failure, and their contempt grew as the ensuing Confederate siege of Chattanooga wore on indecisively. In early October Davis went in person to Bragg's headquarters in the hope of restoring the spirit of the Army of Tennessee. He failed utterly in the attempt. Only the removal of Bragg would have accomplished this object, and it was not done. Bragg offered to resign, but Davis would not permit it; the President must not bow to the dictates of a hostile and irresponsible Congress and press. Bragg remained in command, and Davis returned to Richmond to await the outcome. It was not long delayed. In late November the reinforced Federal army, now commanded by General

The Confederacy

U. S. Grant, attacked the demoralized Confederates on Lookout Mountain and Missionary Ridge and drove them south into Georgia. A campaign begun in bright victory was ended in humiliating defeat, and Davis shared with Bragg the storm of opprobrium that came in its wake.

The Confederacy was grievously crippled and her lines were severed and bent. Federal gunboats patrolled the Mississippi River, cleaving the South in half. So isolated from the main seat of the war was that portion of the Confederacy west of the river that in the summer of 1863 Davis had authorized General E. Kirby Smith, commander of the Trans-Mississippi Department, to take charge of affairs both civil and military in the states of his command. Smith was to follow as closely as possible the policies in effect in the Confederate states east of the river. Davis explained to Congress, "Regular and punctual communication with the Trans-Mississippi is so obstructed as to render difficult a compliance with much of the legislation vesting authority in the executive branch of the Government."

The Trans-Mississippi Department was now virtually autonomous; Southerners waggishly called it Kirby-Smithdom. General Kirby Smith controlled impressment, conscription, Confederate tax collection, cotton exports, transportation, diplomatic missions to Mexico, and the exchange of prisoners of war. Federals held southern Louisiana, northern Arkansas, and the towns of both states along the western bank of the Mississippi River. The interiors of both states were harrowed by guerrilla raids and unsuccessful Northern invasions. Unoccupied by the enemy, Texas produced bountiful crops throughout the conflict and traded briskly with European merchants in Mexico; Texas is said to have had at war's end more hard money than all the rest of the Confederacy. Kirby

A Divided South and Total War

Smith supplied his command by purchasing or impressing cotton and exchanging it for arms and equipment in Mexico. The Trans-Mississippi Department was destined to remain unconquered; it was to outlive briefly the Confederacy itself. But the loss of the Mississippi River denied to the main Southern war effort the great resources of the Southwest.

East of the Mississippi River the Federals held the state of Tennessee; the Confederacy had no army in position to protect the interiors of Mississippi and Alabama from raids of enemy cavalry or to enforce authority there upon a war-weary and bewildered people. The region was a "no-man's land" of dwindling support for the Southern cause. The contiguous effective area of the Confederacy now embraced only the states of the Atlantic seaboard—Virginia, the Carolinas, Georgia, and Florida—plus southern Alabama and eastern Mississippi.

The despair that had overspread the South with the losses at Vicksburg and Gettysburg was immeasurably deepened as the failure at Chattanooga became known. A wise observer in Richmond gave voice to the general sentiment of that city when he wrote, "The crisis of the war is upon us." Mrs. Mary Boykin Chesnut said: "Gloom and unspoken despondency hangs like a pall everywhere." On December 6 a perceptive Southerner wrote with resignation: "Congress meets tomorrow. It has the destinies of the country to dispose of. Is it equal to the emergency? I fear not."

The Congress that assembled on December 7, 1863, was a body of desperate, confused, and bitter men; desperate over the plight of the South, confused in their notions of a remedy, and many of them bitter in their hostility to Davis. Their mood was ripe for measures at once heroic and vindictive; they would call forth a still greater effort and sacrifice from the

The Confederacy

Southern people and at the same time chastise the President for his obstinacy and derelictions. Yet they had no choice but to accept the bulk of the proposals that Davis laid before them, for he spoke convincingly of the perils at hand, and without a coherent program of their own, the lawmakers dared not reject that of the Chief Executive.

The most urgent tangible problem before the Confederacy was the ebbing strength of her armies. The draft laws of 1862 and 1863 had left thousands of able-bodied men at home; many had hired substitutes in their stead, others were enrolled as officers in state guards and hence not subject to Confederate service; and still others were employed in "essential" occupations or holding state and local offices that offered exemption from conscription. Davis asked for a new act that would close the net on these sources of manpower, and in February, 1864, it was passed. Men were now to be drafted from seventeen to fifty years of age, the youngest and oldest of them to be placed in state reserves to relieve men over seventeen and under forty-five for service in the Confederate armies. Every effort was made to eliminate from this law the many objectionable features of the earlier ones. Hiring of substitutes was no longer permitted; the number of offices and occupations providing exemption was drastically reduced; industrial and agricultural workers were to be conscripted and then assigned by the President to necessary war production; and stringent safeguards were fashioned to curb the abuses of the hated provisions relieving slaveowners or overseers.

By early 1864 the Southern armies were perilously wasted from desertion. This is understandable, for no other body of American soldiers ever bore so harsh an ordeal. Demoralized by vital losses in the field and waning faith in their leaders, repudiated by the foreign nations once believed their natural allies, haunted by the knowledge of want and danger to loved ones at home, and worn to the bone by arduous campaigns against superior forces and on woefully short pay, food, and clothing, the fighting men of the Confederacy drifted away from the colors in ever-mounting numbers. In his opening message to Congress, Davis touched upon the darker meaning of these events, saying, "It can no longer be doubted that the zeal with which the people sprang to arms in the beginning of the contest has in some parts of the Confederacy been impaired by the long continuance and magnitude of the struggle." The will to victory was in the ebb.

To staunch the drain of strength from the ranks, Davis urged upon Congress a measure sure to kindle the wrath of many in the South; he asked that the writ of habeas corpus be suspended anew in cases involving desertion, treason, and aid to the enemy. The previous act permitting this had been dead for a year, and countless deserters and shirkers escaped service by appealing to the civil courts. Confederate District Judge James D. Halyburton of Richmond and Associate Justice Richmond M. Pearson of the Supreme Court of North Carolina were the most serious offenders. They opposed conscription on principle and sought to nullify it by freely issuing writs for the release of men seized by provost marshals and conscription officers. Davis deplored the necessity of so stern a measure as suspending the writ, but he believed any other course disastrous and in asking Congress for the act he said,

Desertion, already a frightful evil, will become the order of the day. . . . It [suspension of the writ] is a sharp remedy but a necessary one. . . . It may occasion some clamor; but this will proceed chiefly from the men who have already too long been the active spirits of evil. Loyal citizens will not feel danger, and the disloyal must be made to fear it.

The bill was hotly debated, but on February 15 it became law with many opponents of the administration voting for it.

Closely meshed with the problem of waning morale was that of finance and taxation, for here the Confederacy was most swiftly and surely failing. Revenue from the tax enacted in April, 1863, was soon rendered completely inadequate by evasion of payment, impossibility of collection in areas occupied by the enemy, and especially by the rapid spiral of inflated prices.

Southern farmers resented the tax in kind, claiming injustice in its requirement of a tenth of all their produce while the tax on incomes amounted to only 2 per cent above $1,500. Meetings were held and resolutions passed declaring the agricultural tithe "unjust and tyrannical," and ". . . a relic of barbarism, which alone is practised in the worst of despotism." Collection was difficult under favorable conditions and impossible under any other; areas close to railroads and navigable rivers were obliged to pay heavily, while remote and isolated regions escaped altogether. Perishable goods spoiled in warehouses and on slow and unpredictable trains. During its first year, the tax yielded goods valued at about $40,000,000 according to prevailing prices. Although the tax in kind contributed substantially to the support of Lee's army, it failed to meet the test of modern war.

Merchants and persons on salary were hardly less happy over the other requirements of the existing tax law than were the farmers over the tax in kind. The act was cumbrously drawn and invited evasion. Taxpayers were baffled and angered by complicated provisions for reckoning certain of the taxes on different periods of income, some reaching back as far as a year prior to the passage of the act. The Charleston *Mercury* declared the act unconstitutional, and Robert Toombs said that it was inequitable and unjust and would ". . . gather an abundant harvest of frauds and perjuries." His prediction hit the mark, for the tax was widely flouted; merchants annually selling hundreds of thousands of dollars worth of wares often reported trifling incomes. Though in late April, 1864, Commissioner of Taxes Thompson Allan said that, considering the number of tax districts in enemy hands, the collection of the money tax was "very satisfactory," it actually fell disastrously short of the needs of the Confederacy. At that time it had yielded $82,262,350, scarcely enough to whet the appetite of war.

Unable to meet through current taxes and loans the immense cost of military operations during the summer and fall of 1863, the Treasury Department poured into the already inflated economy of the South an increasing volume of paper currency. When Congress assembled at year's end, more than $700,000,000 was in circulation. Treasury notes were virtually the only purchasing medium of government or citizen and were now worth but a little more than four cents on the dollar. It was said in Richmond, "You take your money to market in the market basket, and bring home what you buy in your pocketbook."

Memminger was desperate. Again he pled for heroic fiscal measures, saying that the public credit could tolerate less than one-third the amount of paper currency then in circulation and that inflation could be cured only through a compulsory funding of the outstanding notes, coupled with a tax on the value of land and slaves, major resources of the South still virtually not taxed. These were momentous issues, for compulsory funding was considered a breach of contract on the part of a government, and a "direct tax" on property was forbidden by the Constitution unless based upon a census and apportioned according to population. Memminger admitted these objections but replied with stern logic, "No contract, however solemn, can require national ruin. . . . The maxim must prevail that the public safety is the supreme law." Many leading newspapers agreed, and Davis strongly indorsed the argument in a message to Congress showing the impossibility of taking a census at the time and demonstrating the absurdity of following the letter of the Constitution to the destruction of the republic.

The legislators were persuaded. On February 17, 1864, they enacted a law requiring outstanding treasury notes to be exchanged for twenty-year bonds bearing 4 per cent interest or for new notes of one-third lower denomination payable two years after the end of the war. An ad valorem tax of 5 per cent was placed on land and slaves, along with taxes of varying amount on a wide assortment of other property and assets, including gold and silver plate and coin, gold dust, shares in corporations, and bank credits. An additional loan of $500,000,000 was authorized to be made in thirty-year bonds bearing 6 per cent interest. But Congress lacked the fortitude and wisdom to adopt a full-muscled tax law, and many crippling provisions were allowed. The agricultural tithe and income tax were both renewed but were deductible from the other taxes, thus greatly reducing the revenue available from them. Even more serious, the tax on land and slaves was based on prewar valuation and was payable in the new treasury notes in which the old currency was being funded. Hence the primary sources of Southern wealth remained favored assets, taxable only in depreciated paper money and never called upon to support their share of the burden of war.

The various measures of early 1864 designed to strengthen the Confederacy came of a forced and unhappy union of President and Congress. Even as these laws were debated, others were being fashioned for the purpose of reducing Davis' authority and humiliating him before the country. Certain congressmen talked of elevating Lee to the position of general in chief, and as an apparent preliminary to this the Senate passed resolutions praising the Virginian for his conduct of military operations. Led by Foote, the House of Representatives assailed with increased ardor the competence of Commissary General Northrop, and again Davis withstood all attempts to compel the dismissal of this unpopular officer. A bitter feud was waged between Congress and the Chief Executive over the appointment of a new Quartermaster General. In August, 1863, Davis had removed Abraham C. Myers from the office and had named Brigadier General Alexander R. Lawton as his successor; but the Senate now withheld Lawton's confirmation and voted that Myers still held the post. Davis rightly declared this unconstitutional and with great difficulty succeeded in keeping Lawton in the position. A biographer of Davis has said of these attacks upon him, "The jackals turned on the sick lion."

But the sick lion invited attack, for Davis did things that he must have known would madden the opposition and cripple the prestige of the administration. After winning the contest to retain Lawton as Quartermaster General, Davis rubbed salt into the wound by ordering Myers to resume duty as a colonel in the very department that he had run since the beginning of the war. Next came the promotion of General Bragg. After withdrawing the shattered Army of Tennessee into northern Georgia, Bragg had again asked to be relieved of command. This time the cabinet insisted that the resignation be accepted, and it was done. Joseph E. Johnston was placed in command of the Army of Tennessee. But Bragg was not reduced and humiliated as Rhett, Pollard, Wigfall, and a host of others would have had it. Instead, he was brought to Richmond as military adviser to the President with general supervision of the conduct of Confederate armies. Pollard spoke for multitudes of outraged Southerners with this bitter line in the Richmond *Examiner*, "From Lookout Mountain, a step to the highest honor and power is natural and inevitable." The flawed stone had been made head of the corner.

The battle of Chattanooga was followed by a lull in campaigning as both antagonists girded themselves for the supreme effort—as the North summoned strength to trample out the last sparks of Southern resistance, and the South prepared to exact such toll in blood and treasure that the Northern people would yet despair of victory and assent to Confederate independence. The thriving industry and economy of the North were geared to full production and her veteran army of nearly one million men was now under the unified command of General Grant and poised for the decisive thrust. Grant's strategy was that of massive attrition; Lincoln touched the key to its success in the statement, "It is the dogged pertinacity of the man that wins." Grant would attack remorselessly on all fronts at once, forcing the Confederacy to fight without respite until her resources were spent and her spirit crushed. Then the war would be over.

The Confederacy was fearfully hurt by blows from without and dissension within; but she was still dangerous, as the speared tiger is dangerous. In spite of widespread antipathy to Davis, he still remained an example of unyielding defiance against the foe; and in spite of defeat at Gettysburg, Lee was still the South's paladin of the battlefield. After three years of war such as the world had seldom seen, the Army of Northern Virginia still stood gaunt and formidable across the familiar invasion paths that led to Richmond. While this army endured the Confederacy would live.

Armed with more stringent laws for mobilizing the resources of the South, Confederate leaders in early 1864 set about to replenish the shrinking armies and restore the will for victory. There were elements of strength and efficiency in the midst of weakness and confusion. Production of arms and munitions was now one of the brightest aspects of the Southern war effort, for the superb planning and organization of Chief of Ordnance Josiah Gorgas and of individual enterprisers such as General Joseph R. Anderson had borne fruit. Cannon, rifles, pistols, sabers, ammunition, and the sundry paraphernalia of war came in abundance from more than a dozen busy government arsenals scattered from Richmond to Selma, Alabama. Anderson's great Tredegar Works clanged and glowed the day around with the forging of its deadly wares. As the conflict reached its climax Gorgas could say with pride and a good measure of accuracy, "Where three years ago we were not making a gun, a pistol nor a sabre, no shot nor shell (except at the Tredegar Works)—a pound of powder—we now make all these in quantities to meet the demands of our large armies."

Notwithstanding this forgivable boast, the Confederacy fell short of full self-sufficiency in arms and supplies. To the vital quantities being fashioned in her own factories was added an increasing amount of equipment from abroad. For the Southern coastline was only imperfectly guarded and swift blockade-runners found their way through the Union navy. More than six hundred vessels at various times participated in this trade. A majority of them belonged to private individuals and companies and were of European registry, but from the beginning a number of ships of the Confederate government were committed to this venture. The enterprising General Gorgas of the Ordnance Bureau led the way. Gorgas purchased cotton in the South and sent it through the blockade to Fraser, Trenholm and Company in Liverpool or to some other English firm, who for a profit exchanged the cotton for industrial goods. Following Gorgas' success, other government agencies took up the practice.

Davis was lamentably slow to approve government blockade-running, for he considered it an admission of the general effectiveness of the blockade and hence incompatible with the claim of Confederate diplomats that the blockade was of paper. But the diplomatic game was now almost up; hope for British recognition was virtually abandoned, and overtures to France were based upon Napoleon's hunger for Mexico. Military and medical supplies were more imperative than the subtleties of statecraft.

Early in 1864, Congress gave the President sole authority over the shipment of cotton and at the same time required private blockade-runners to place one-half their cargo space at the disposal of the government, on fixed rates. Already Benjamin had appointed a co-ordinator of Confederate overseas purchasing. Presently a Bureau of Foreign Supplies was established to buy and ship cotton for the Confederacy. The system worked remarkably and for the remainder of the war provided the hard-pressed South with many of the civilian and military necessities that could not be manufactured at home. During the last three months of 1864, the South received through the blockade 500,000 pairs of shoes, 800,000 pounds of bacon, 2,000,000 pounds of saltpeter, 316,000 blankets, 69,000 rifles, and various other supplies. Professor Owsley has aptly said that having failed as sovereign of the world, cotton at last found its true role as the economic servant of the Confederacy.

Southern agriculture retained much of its vitality as the war entered the final year. Armies might retreat and cities fall, but the land was still favored of sun and rain, and in areas beyond the invaders' reach fields were tilled by the wives and children of absent farmers and by obedient plantation slaves. Harvests were bountiful. Little cotton was planted now, but instead an abundance of corn, sweet potatoes, peas, beans, sorghum, oats, hay, and orchard fruits. Beef, pork, and poultry were plentiful, and woods and streams teemed with game. There was food enough in the South for soldiers and civilian population alike.

But the fundamental weaknesses of Confederate industry and supply were not mastered by the achievements of Gorgas and Anderson, the blockade-runners, and the tillers of the soil. For the shortcomings were many and of a nature peculiarly vulnerable to the unremitting warfare that Grant proposed to wage upon the South. The silent grip of the Federal navy grew ever tighter and the number of captures among blockade-runners steadily mounted. Still more significant, Southern ports were avoided altogether by the major cargo vessels of the world. By 1864 the blockade was strangling the Southern economy. Perhaps few scholars today would accept Professor Nathaniel W. Stephenson's statement that the Confederacy was destroyed by the blockade, but certainly all would agree that it immeasurably reduced her capacity to resist.

The Confederacy

To the paralyzing influence of the blockade was added that of lamed internal communications. Wanting adequate facilities for the manufacture and repair of locomotives and rails, the Confederacy now found her transportation taxed beyond endurance. Feeble and dilapidated engines and cars crept laboriously over outworn rails in a vain effort to move troops and supplies to points of greatest need. Less-important lines were torn up and their rails used to maintain the essential ones, but these and other desperate improvisations were unavailing. Other difficulties arose out of the industrial retardation of the South; frequently the gauges of different railways failed to match, and time-consuming transfers of freight were required. Owners and managers of various lines often refused to co-ordinate their efforts, and Confederate authorities lacked the power to force them to do so. Shortages of wagons, carts, and livestock further impaired the mobility of a war-pressed agrarian society. Depots and warehouses were often stacked high with provisions while troops and urban dwellers suffered acute hunger and exposure. Confederate communications were unequal to the exigencies of total war.

On May 4, 1864, Grant sent the Army of the Potomac southward across the Rapidan River and at the same time wired General William T. Sherman to move upon Johnston in Georgia. General Nathaniel Banks had already attacked in Louisiana; the Union commanders in the Shenandoah Valley and on the James River of Virginia were now ordered forward against Confederate positions and lines of supply. The strategy of massive attrition was under way.

Now began the most furious sustained fighting of the war. On May 5 Lee opened the battle of the Wilderness in an area filled with dense woods and the ghosts of Chancellorsville. After three days of carnage Grant drew off, but he did not abandon the campaign. Instead, he moved southeastward around the Confederate right flank. There followed a month of continuous marching and combat, with Grant circling relentlessly left and forward and Lee maneuvering brilliantly to keep his thin gray line always between Richmond and the foe. The Wilderness had left Lee too weak to attack, and he now unfailingly fought from behind earthworks. At Spotsylvania Court House (May 8–18) and Cold Harbor (June 1–3) Grant was bloodily repulsed in powerful assaults upon the Confederate positions. The Northern commander had written on May 11, "I propose to fight it out on this line if it takes all summer." But the slaughter of Cold Harbor changed his mind; on June 14 he crossed the James River and swung completely around the Confederate capital so as to approach it from the south. For once Lee failed to read his opponent's mind. Except for Beauregard's heroic stand at Petersburg against overwhelming numbers, Richmond would then have fallen. Lee's troops joined those of Beauregard on June 18 and the great siege of the war was on.

As the armies in Virginia locked in mortal combat, Sherman struck for Atlanta, advancing along the Western and Atlantic Railroad and maneuvering skilfully right and left in an effort to flank his opponent and destroy him. Johnston gave ground slowly, parried masterfully, and husbanded his troops for a decisive counterstroke the moment his adversary's guard was relaxed. Sherman found every move blocked by entrenchments, and his attacks on Resaca (May 13–15), New Hope Church (May 25–27) and Kenesaw Mountain (June 27) were repulsed with severe loss. But always Johnston retreated. Early July found Johnston in the earthworks before Atlanta, with this important Georgia rail center under siege.

The other offensives in Grant's broad strategy were quickly blunted. In April two Union thrusts west of the Mississippi were stopped: General Richard Taylor smashed Banks' Red River campaign in western Louisiana; and General Kirby Smith defeated a movement by General Frederick Steele from Arkansas upon northern Louisiana. On May 15 the Union advance up the Shenandoah Valley was stopped at New Market, Virginia, by Generals Breckinridge and Imboden and the cadets of the Virginia Military Institute. Five days later General Benjamin F. Butler was attacked by Beauregard below Richmond and thrust back into the Bermuda Hundred, a pocket between the James and Appomattox rivers. There, according to Grant's description, Butler was "corked up like a cork in a bottle."

Thus at mid-summer the war again seemed stalemated, with the end nowhere in sight. Grant's casualties since crossing the Rapidan had been fearful, and even now he was farther from Richmond than McClellan had been in the summer of 1862. Sherman was lodged in the depths of Georgia, possibly facing disaster. Southern morale rose faintly with these developments, and the people of the North were filled with despondency, and many began to urge peace at any price. This became the vital issue of the presidential election to be held in the North in November. The Democratic convention meeting in Chicago in August nominated General McClellan for President and wrote a platform to end hostilities, then seek a reunion through peaceable means. Confederate agents Clement C. Clay and Jacob Thompson in Canada were in touch with leaders of the Northern peace movement, who assured the Southerners that the Democrats, if victorious, would permit the Confederacy to go her way. So widespread was demoralization in the North that on August 23 Lincoln wrote glumly, "It seems exceedingly probable that this administration will not be re-elected."

But the true omens portended a different end. For attrition had done its work; behind her frayed armies the Confederacy was sinking fast. Her losses in the great campaigns of the spring and summer had been cruel and could not be replaced. Deadlier than battle casualties were the internal wounds that now opened under Grant's hammer strokes. Discord and confusion mounted as the advocates of both state rights and Unionism (or pacifism) challenged the efforts of Confederate authorities to direct the total resources of the land into a resistance unto death.

The leading spirit of both opposition movements was the sickly and embittered Vice President of the Confederacy Alexander Stephens, for he was blinded by a curious political schizophrenia to the incompatibility of state rights and Unionism. Stephens had long ago broken irreparably with the Davis administration and had returned to Georgia to lead that state's trio of obstructionists (Stephens himself, Governor Brown, and Toombs) in their baleful designs. The government's every measure born of the extremity of early 1864—conscription, impressment, taxation, and suspension of the writ of habeas corpus—was relentlessly attacked. Addressing the Georgia legislature, Stephens denounced these acts as final steps toward military despotism and cried, "Could dictatorial power be more complete?" Under the spell of such oratory the legislators passed resolutions threatening the secession of Georgia from the Confederacy.

Nor were the Georgia state rightists alone; they appealed

to sentiments deeply rooted in the Southern heart. On countless specific issues the governors or legislatures of most of the states opposed the extension of central authority. Governor Vance of North Carolina fully rivaled the Georgians in this conviction, which hardened as the war took increasing toll of the men and materials of his state. He insisted that each state equip its own troops in the Confederate army and refused to permit Confederate agents to purchase supplies of clothing, blankets, shoes, tents, and harness made in the many factories of North Carolina. When Congress required one-half the cargo space on blockade-runners, Vance refused to comply on vessels in which his government owned interest, and replied in wrath, "Is it possible that such an unblushing outrage is intended by the government? I have no comment to make on such proceedings further than that I will fire the ships before I will agree to it." Governors Thomas H. Watts of Alabama and Charles Clark of Mississippi took a similar attitude on the general question of state supply, as of course did Brown of Georgia. Ultimately even Governor John Milton of Florida was forced in self-defense to follow suit, though he had supported Confederate control throughout most of the war. As Lee's veterans marched barefoot in the snow of Virginia, their apparel tattered to the point of embarrassing exposure, the state governments hoarded vast supplies of shoes, uniforms, and blankets against the future needs of their own troops. At the end of the war Vance could point with pernicious pride to warehouses in Richmond, Raleigh, and elsewhere holding 92,000 uniforms and comparable stores of blankets and leather belonging to the state of North Carolina.

President Davis passed fair judgment upon the extreme practitioners of state rights when in December of 1864 he wrote:

A Divided South and Total War

The difficulties with which this Government has to contend in opposing with its limited resources the devastating tide of invasion which the power of our enemy is pouring upon us would be great enough under any circumstances and with the most united and harmonious action of our whole people. But those difficulties have been materially increased by the persistent interference of some of the State authorities—legislative, executive, and judicial—hindering the action of this Government, obstructing the execution of its laws, denouncing its necessary policy, impairing its hold upon the confidence of the people, and dealing with it rather as if it were the public enemy than the Government which they themselves had established for the common defense and which was their only hope for safety from the untold horrors of Yankee despotism.

The chief victim of state-rights intransigence was the supreme instrument of Confederate survival—the Confederate army. Men continued to be hoarded, as did supplies, with each state maintaining its own sizable military establishment. All efforts by the central government to draw the residue of able-bodied men of the South into a unified striking force were obstructed by exemption from conscription. Countless state civil and military officials were kept beyond the reach of the enrolling officers. North Carolina led the way, withholding an estimated 15,000 to 20,000 men in 1864; but Georgia was close behind, and Mississippi, Alabama, Virginia, and South Carolina followed the same course, though less extensively. It was said facetiously of this practice in Georgia, "Every private in Joe Brown's militia holds an officer's commission." To the desperate authorities in Richmond, this was too nearly true to be amusing.

So widespread and vehement in 1864 was denunciation of the suspension of the writ of habeas corpus that Davis forbore to apply it save under direst provocation, and Congress would not renew the act when it expired in August. Shirkers and deserters were thus assured of protection in the civil courts, and in innumerable cases they met with no disappointment. Confederate Superintendent of Conscription John S. Preston gave voice to despair, "From one end of the Confederacy to the other every constituted authority, every officer, every man and woman is engaged in opposing the enrolling officer in the execution of his duties."

Scarcely less deadly to the Confederate war effort than state-rights dissidence was the burgeoning spirit of pacifism among the war-stricken population. From the numerous Unionists and others of lukewarm zeal for independence now arose the cry for peace. It had been sounded as early as 1862 in the mountainous districts of North Carolina, Tennessee, Alabama, and Arkansas; and in 1863 it was openly proclaimed in the columns of the Raleigh, North Carolina, *Standard* by the Unionist editor William W. Holden. For some time Alexander Stephens had toyed with the idea of leading a peace movement to reunite the warring peoples, and he had once proposed to the Confederate Senate the calling of a convention of all the states, North and South, to attempt this. He fatuously believed that the war could be ended and the Union restored, and at the same time the principle of state rights be preserved.

In December, 1863, Lincoln set forth a plan for bringing the seceded states back into their places in the Union. He offered amnesty to all citizens who would swear allegiance to the Union, and readmission to any state in which 10 per cent of the voters of 1860 had taken the oath and had formed a loyal government. This plan was to the embattled and weakening South what Wilson's Fourteen Points later were designed to be to a demoralized Germany. It offered instant peace, easy and without vengeance, and it was grist for the mills of Southern pacifists. Holden responded to Lincoln's inducement. In the spring of 1864 he ran against Vance for the governorship of North Carolina, with peace as his platform. Holden was defeated at the polls and the peace movement abated during the summer as the great Federal offensives appeared stalled before Petersburg and Atlanta. But the vote in the North Carolina election had shown that the peace urge ran strong there. It was almost as strong in other parts of the Confederacy.

State rightists and pacifists mingled their voices with the long-sustained chorus of hostility to the administration. The Charleston *Mercury* and Richmond *Examiner* intensified their campaign of vituperation, illogically blending charges of impotence with charges of tyranny. Robert Barnwell Rhett was no longer active. He had tasted defeat in his own state in the congressional election of the preceding autumn and was now virtually in retirement, plagued with a cancerous growth on his face. The *Mercury* likened him to the "Saviour of the world [who] was rejected of men"; then said sadly, "Those who made this revolution do not direct it." Editor Robert Barnwell Rhett, Jr., carried on in his father's tradition of intemperance. More ominous than the antipathy of ancient enemies was the falling away of erstwhile friends; newspapers such as the Charleston *Courier* that had faithfully supported Davis through his countless vicissitudes now turned cool toward him. Distrust of the government overspread the Confederacy.

Desertion from the Southern armies rose disastrously with the mounting fury of the war. Cowards fled from the constant prospect of death, and the weak broke under the indescribable hardships and privations of the field. Unionists who had been conscripted into service against their will took advantage of the weakening of Confederate authority in remote areas and of the legalisms of state-rights judges and other officials to leave the ranks and defy provost marshals sent to retrieve them. Veterans who had endured three years of travail and hazard grew confused and lost faith as they heard their leaders denounced for incompetence and for yearning after military despotism or as they were told that an honorable peace was theirs for the asking. Even the lion-hearted yielded to desperate entreaties from home and the news that wives and children were at death's door. Absenteeism, disease, and battle casualties alike ravaged the defending armies at Petersburg and Atlanta as Grant and Sherman massed their columns for the kill.

The people of Georgia were overcome with agony and panic as Sherman drove irresistibly into the heart of the state. Frantically, some of them called upon Davis for reinforcements and for the replacement of General Johnston with a commander who would stand and fight and give up no more of the precious soil of Georgia. Davis had never fully trusted Johnston, and the President's vexation had grown with every step in the long retreat. A decisive Confederate victory was imperative, thought Davis; it would rekindle Southern morale and perhaps defeat Lincoln at the polls and place the peace party of the North in the ascendancy.

On July 17, Davis took the fateful step of removing the Fabian Johnston from command of the Army of Tennessee and replacing him with General John Bell Hood. No soldier of the Confederacy was more famed as a fighter than was the towering Hood; an arm disabled at Gettysburg and the stump of a leg lost at Chickamauga gave proof of his redoubtable courage. Poet Stephen Vincent Benét has likened him to a "berserk sword." Everyone, including Sherman, knew that Hood's elevation to command was the signal for attack.

A Divided South and Total War

Three days later Hood struck. For six weeks he hammered, feinted, and flanked against the constricting coils of Sherman's army in the battles of Peach Tree Creek (July 20), Atlanta (July 22), Ezra Church (July 28), and Jonesboro (August 31–September 1). The grappling armies described a complete semicircle around Atlanta, from north to south of the city. But Hood's furious assaults were of no avail. He had attempted the virtually impossible—the destruction of a force twice the size of his own. Instead of destroying the foe, Hood had fought his own troops to exhaustion. On September 2 he extricated his battered army and withdrew to the south. That day Sherman took Atlanta.

IX

A Beleaguered People

The people of the Confederacy lived intimately with war. For four years war was among them, in their homes, in their churches, in their schools, in their fields, and in their woods and streams. With its pomp and glory, war stirred the folk of the South to great enthusiasm and strenuous endeavor, and it saddened and humbled them with its waste of their sons and substance. War left its physical scars on the face of the land and its more enduring psychic scars within the hearts of the people. War filled the tissues of Southern life.

Spirits were high in the South at the first call to arms, for only a few sensed the magnitude of the conflict. Margaret Mitchell's youthful hotspurs in *Gone with the Wind*, whooping exultantly over the outbreak of war, are faithful representations of many flesh-and-blood Southerners of 1861. A majority of Confederates looked upon the Yankees as a money-grubbing race too spineless to withstand the test of war. Men of wisdom who warned against this false optimism were waved aside as misguided prophets of doom, and Southern victory at First Manassas seemed to demonstrate conclusively the invincibility of Confederate arms.

Thus the South went larking off to war. Throughout 1861 the land was alive with the mustering of state militia organizations and the formation of volunteer regiments. All possible forces of society were turned to the support of the war effort. Parades, barbecues, and speakings were held, and distinguished citizens exhorted the young men to come to the colors. Planters, merchants, and others of means pledged handsome sums for the purchase of uniforms and equipment. Social affairs became occasions for sustaining the Confederacy. Balls were given with admission charged and the proceeds turned over to military organizations; auctions, bazaars, musicals, tableaux, and candy-pullings were held and the profits donated for the procurement of arms and supplies; sewing societies were formed among the women to make clothing for the troops; and young girls busied themselves with picking lint and making bandages. Southern arms were backed by a great, spontaneous folk movement.

Early in the war there was a measure of gaiety even amid the customarily sad departure of soldiers for the front. Regiments preparing to board trains or steamboats bound for Kentucky and Virginia were honored with sermons, band performances, and gala flag presentations. These ceremonies were the more memorable because the flags usually were made by women of the community—mothers, wives, and sweethearts of the departing men—and were presented by the prettiest of the local belles. War had not yet come home to the people of the South.

But war in its severity was not long delayed. By 1862 most Southern ports lay idle, large numbers of men were away in the armies and unable to till their farms, and the previous season's crops were without markets. At the same time, the South's supply of manufactured goods dwindled, and the prices of imported necessities soared. Presently the difficulties were compounded by inflation of the Confederate currency and by the hoarding and speculation that came in its wake. Farm implements, shoes, clothing, and drugs were soon beyond the financial reach of a great majority of the inhabitants of the South. The penalty of sustaining an agrarian economy in an industrial age was now to be paid in toil and privation.

For most of the civilian population of the South the last three years of the war were years of indescribable hardship. Confederate conscription laws permitted no exemptions on account of dependents, and innumerable heads of families were called into military service. Wives and children were thus left unassisted to the rigors of privation and inflation, the perils of invasion and possible slave insurrection, and the unremitting toil of making crops and maintaining households. The fortitude of these folk has seldom if ever been surpassed. The land was tilled and the embattled South was fed; hides were tanned and shoes made; thread was spun, cloth woven, and garments sewn; and innumerable substitutes and improvisations were adopted for the goods and implements that no longer could be purchased.

On plantations and farms not in the path of Federal invasion, food was plentiful, though usually crude and less tasty than before the war. Cornmeal replaced flour; sorghum molasses took the place of sugar and sugar syrup, except in the Louisiana cane country; salt became exceedingly dear as the Confederacy was forced to rely upon her own mines, salt springs, and the evaporation of sea water for this seasoning and preservative; and such luxuries as coffee virtually disappeared. Sweet potatoes, field peas, cornbread, and pork were the almost universal diet of the rural South during the war. To the masses of the small farmers and Negro slaves this brought no great discomfort, for it was essentially what they had always eaten.

Wherever the armies went the land was stripped of much of its sustenance, and before the coming of peace the armies had moved over vast areas of the South. Whether the Federals plundered out of a compulsion to punish a rebellious people, out of hunger, or out of sheer deviltry, the result was the same. Whether the looters wore the blue or the gray, the result was still the same, for Confederate soldiers as well as Yankees often foraged without restraint. Late in the war Confederate General Joseph Wheeler's cavalry was thought by the residents of Georgia to be as severe in their depredations as the invaders. Crops were seized by the soldiers of both armies, corn cribs and smokehouses were emptied, and horses, cattle, hogs, and poultry were taken from their owners. Citizens in the track of the campaigns were left at starvation's door.

As the Northern armies thrust into the Confederacy many planters abandoned their homes and withdrew to areas temporarily beyond the invaders' reach, taking with them their slaves and whatever part of their produce and other valuables that could be transported. Thousands of Southern refugees ultimately made their way to Texas. The exodus of these people from their habitations had much of the appearance of comparable flights in the wars of the twentieth century. Roads were jammed with wagons and carts piled high with family belongings, and most of the exiles, both black and white, trudged along the sides. Organized into caravans for comfort and protection, the fugitives moved laboriously by day and camped under the stars at night. The physical and mental pain endured by these weary folk could hardly be exaggerated. All had abandoned homes to the vandalism of the Negroes and soldiers and to the ruin that comes of neglect. None knew what the morrow held in store. Women and children suffered most acutely from the exposure and privation of the long march. The uprooted of the Confederacy knew the full meaning of war.

Southerners who owned no land were the most sorely pinched of all. Countless families of rural tenants and urban laborers endured severe hunger and exposure throughout most of the war. Whether the breadwinners were in uniform or detailed to labor in essential industries, their wages were but a pittance before the soaring inflation. When in Richmond in 1863 butter cost $4.00 a pound, calico $4.50 a yard, and coal $1.25 a bushel, private soldiers of the Confederacy were receiving $11.00 a month, and workers in Southern armories were being paid $3.00 a day. Entire families lived in a single room, huddled around a fireplace that served both for cooking victuals and warming their bodies. Corn fritters and boiled potatoes and beans were their usual fare. As the war continued, wages progressively fell farther behind advancing prices, and the Confederacy became a land of widespread want and suffering.

Though many of the commodities denied by war to the folk of the South were luxuries, many also were necessities, and some were vital to life itself. Medicine was perhaps the dearest item in the Confederacy. As early as 1862 quinine was being sold for $20.00 an ounce in Louisiana, and two years later it was $100.00 an ounce. To the masses of the people it was utterly unobtainable. In a region traditionally plagued with malaria this was a cruel loss. The Confederate government established numerous medical laboratories, and various substitutes for imported drugs were fashioned out of common roots and herbs. At least one planter stretched his precious supply of smallpox vaccine by using the vaccination scabs from his own family to inoculate his slaves. A profusion of nostrums and useless remedies appeared. Inhaling the aroma of burnt leather was supposed to prevent smallpox; and diphtheria was thought to be curable by smearing the patient with lard and administering heavy doses of calomel twice a day. The wartime South suffered no general epidemic of disease for lack of drugs, but many localities were swept with typhoid fever, pneumonia, smallpox, malaria, whooping cough, and measles. Thousands of civilians in the Confederacy must have perished for want of drugs and adequate medical care.

Providing relief for those impoverished or disabled by war was looked upon as a patriotic duty, and the Southern people gave generously for the wives and children of soldiers who could not support them. Innumerable individuals donated goods and services to the families of the less fortunate; benevolent societies were formed and charity markets established by them in all major cities to receive and dispense free of charge the produce contributed by neighboring planters. State and local governments appropriated money for the subsistence of soldiers' dependents. But the needy became countless as the conflict lengthened and the South was overtaken by calamity. Probably no system of relief would have been adequate to the needs of a people thus stricken. The Confederate government attempted none, for to have done so would have been considered an unconstitutional aggrandizement of central authority. At the height of the war, destitution in the Confederacy went largely unabated.

Mental anguish bore as heavily as physical hardship upon the home population of the Confederacy. A great loneliness came upon communities and families after most of their men had gone to the front, and in areas where Negroes were numerous this feeling was deepened by the dread of servile insurrection. Mail was slow and irregular, and in the last months of the war letters often required weeks to reach their destinations. Plantations and farms were isolated in normal times, and now they became places of maddening seclusion. A plantation mistress recalled living for a long period without any word of the outside world, only to discover that in the meantime close friends and relatives had died and been buried without her knowing it. A lonely planter wrote with emotion, "Solitude is not good for man." But solitude was inescapable in the rural expanses of the Confederacy.

Infinitely more cruel than loneliness was the grief caused by the death of sons and husbands in uniform. As the war continued and grew in severity, the South was filled with widows and families in bereavement. One-fourth of the able-bodied men of the Confederacy died during the war. Thousands of women who a short time earlier had worn bridal gowns or the gay apparel of the ballroom were now arrayed in the somber black of mourning. A heart-broken mother wrote, "Every breeze chants the requiem of dying heroes." A Louisiana girl living as a refugee in Texas penned in her diary, "Never a letter but brings news of death." Mrs. Mary Boykin Chesnut claimed that grief and anxiety killed nearly as many Southern women as did Northern bullets kill Southern men. The South became a land of sorrow.

The Confederacy was as faithfully served by the cultural and intellectual resources of the South as by her material resources. Southern literature was profoundly touched by the movement for independence and the war, and the people's deep emotions found expression in a great outpouring of poetry. Most of the poetry was bad—trite and excessively sentimental. But there was gold among the dross: many Southerners wrote patriotic verse of enduring quality.

Henry Timrod and Paul Hamilton Hayne were inspired to distinguished poetic achievement by their zeal for the Southern cause and their admiration for Confederate valor on the battlefield. The two were personal friends and both were members of a small group of writers that before the war had surrounded the noted Charleston literary figure, William Gilmore Simms. Timrod became the "Poet laureate of the Confederacy." In "The Cotton Boll" he extolled the virtues of the South through the symbolism of her famed agricultural plant; in "Ethnogenesis" he hailed the Confederacy as the domain of a superior race and culture. "A Cry to Arms" was Timrod's stirring affirmation of defiance against the North. Hayne paid tribute to Southern prowess in numerous poems, including "Our Martyrs" and his finest wartime composition "The Battle of Charleston Harbor." After the war Timrod wrote his "Ode" to the Confederate dead buried in the Magnolia Cemetery of Charleston, eulogizing them in lines of surpassing beauty and pathos as "martyrs to a fallen cause."

Many less-gifted poets also captured the Southern spirit in verse. Francis Orray Ticknor of Georgia praised the Virginia soldiers in "Virginians of the Valley" and touched the hearts of Southern readers with "Little Giffen" (of Tennessee) telling of the death in combat of a youthful drummer boy. Father Abram J. Ryan, a Catholic chaplain in the Southern army, later composed the two most popular poems written about the Confederacy—"The Sword of Robert E. Lee" and "The Conquered

Banner." James Ryder Randall's "Maryland, My Maryland" was a fiery denunciation of Northern aggression.

Confederate fiction lacked both the emotional depth and literary skill of the poems of Timrod and Hayne. The South's greatest ante-bellum novelist, William Gilmore Simms, was unable to rise to the challenge of the war. He wrote some patriotic verse and a number of spirited editorials supporting the Southern cause. But the epochal novel of the Confederacy that might have flowered out of his great talent was not written. The outstanding war novel produced in the Confederacy was *Macaria; or, Altars of Sacrifice* by Augusta Jane Evans of Mobile, later to become nationally famous for her book *St. Elmo*. *Macaria* is a story of pure love frustrated by family antagonisms and ended in the hero's death on the battlefield. It expounds Southern political and social philosophy as well as the author's belief that the people of the South ought to follow the example of the ancient Greek heroine Macaria and immolate themselves upon the altar of patriotism.

Other Southern writers, such as John Esten Cooke of Virginia and George Washington Cable of Louisiana, gained experiences in the war that later would inspire one of America's most enduring literary genres—the Confederate novel. In *Surry of Eagle's Nest* (1866) and *The Wearing of the Gray* (1867) Cooke planted the seeds that one day would mature in Stark Young's *So Red the Rose* and Margaret Mitchell's *Gone with the Wind*.

Journalism during the war retained the fire and individuality that had made it the most virile form of ante-bellum Southern literature. With rare exception, the Southern press supported the war for independence, and many leading journals favored the Davis administration. Foremost among these were the

A Beleaguered People

Richmond *Enquirer*, the Richmond *Sentinel*, and Richard Yeadon's Charleston *Courier*, all considered unofficial organs of the government. Yet one of the ironies of Confederate history lies in the part played by Southern editors in destroying the Confederacy. Newspapers were not suppressed by the Confederate government even when they advocated pacifism or the most extreme interpretations of state rights, nor when they accused the Davis administration of incompetence and military despotism. Pollard and Daniel of the Richmond *Examiner* and Rhett through the columns of the Charleston *Mercury* were major offenders in blighting the confidence and morale of the Southern people. Freedom of the press was a dubious blessing to an infant nation fighting for survival.

Confederate literature that was destined to achieve the most lasting fame was not the work of professional writers, but of a number of talented amateurs—mostly women—who kept diaries or wrote memoirs of their experiences and observations during the war. Classic among these is the diary of Mrs. Mary Boykin Chesnut, whose husband was a former United States Senator and a military aide to President Davis. Published after the war under the title *A Diary from Dixie*, it is the most readable and one of the most authentic of all commentaries on life and death in the embattled South. Comparable works are *Diary of a Southern Refugee* by Judith White McGuire, *A Confederate Girl's Diary* by Sarah Morgan Dawson, and *Brockenburn* by Sarah Katherine Stone.

In spite of the fervor of Confederate nationalism and the strivings of Southern authors toward cultural autonomy, the Confederacy was unable to escape the literary dependence of the ante-bellum South. Southern readers customarily had ignored their own writers and had turned instead to the novels, biographies, and historical treatises written by Northerners and Europeans. Confederate readers largely did the same. Works of Shakespeare, Scott, Dickens, Tennyson, Hugo, and Dumas were highly favored in the wartime South, and a plantation girl of literary taste admitted in her diary: "We hope Mr. McGee [a friend] will be able to get *Harper's* to us. . . . The literature of the North is to us what the 'flesh pots of Egypt' were to the wandering Israelites—we long for it."

Of the fine arts, music most deeply touched the masses of the Confederacy. Drama flourished in Richmond and Charleston, much of it patriotic in nature, and some of more conventional theme; and Southern painters and sculptors turned to Confederate leaders as their subjects. But these were forms of artistic expression that appealed to a select few; music of one kind or another was enjoyed by all Southerners, and the Confederacy drew upon a wide variety of melodies for a body of patriotic music that was unexcelled in spirit and tempo. A minstrel song named "Dixie," written by Daniel Emmett of Ohio, became the "national anthem" of the South. An Irish immigrant, Harry McCarthy, gave the Confederacy "The Bonnie Blue Flag," with its bold verse and lilting martial air. "Maryland, My Maryland" was set to the tune of an old German song to become the "Marseillaise" of the Confederacy. An amorous and jaunty minstrel lyric, "The Yellow Rose of Texas," was converted into a favorite marching song of the Southern army. "Lorena" and "Somebody's Darling" accurately rendered a sentimental people's emotions of love and sorrow in the travail of war. Music was a potent stimulant to the spirit of the wartime South.

A major buttress of the Confederacy was religion. The mind of the Old South was wrought largely of orthodox Christianity;

theologians had formed the vanguard of secession. The Confederate war effort received the unstinting support of the Southern clergy. Setting the example were such eminent religious leaders as Dr. James H. Thornwell, President of South Carolina College, Professor Robert Louis Dabney of the Columbia Theological Seminary, and Pastor Benjamin M. Palmer of the First Presbyterian Church of New Orleans. Expounding the righteousness of the Southern cause, thousands of ministers of the Gospel urged members of their congregations to selfless sacrifice in behalf of the Confederacy. God would uphold the arms of the faithful against Northern infidelity, the people of the South were assured, and they believed that it was true. Churchmen "sounded the trumpets" that led the South to war.

Southerners of all faiths were loyal to the Confederacy. Before the war Southern Methodists and Baptists had withdrawn from fellow believers of the North; now Southern Episcopalians, Presbyterians, and Lutherans broke ties with Northern communicants and established independent churches. As part of a world-wide ecclesiastical system, Southern Catholics could not form a separate Confederate church; nevertheless, they upheld the cause of the South with unsurpassed zeal.

Religion affected the lives of the high and the humble alike. President Davis was converted to the Episcopal faith shortly after his inauguration. The South's greatest generals, Lee and Jackson, were devout Christians, and many other famed soldiers were churchmen. Robert Louis Dabney served on Jackson's staff; Lee's chief of artillery, General W. M. Pendleton, was an Episcopal minister; Lieutenant General Leonidas Polk was Episcopal Bishop of Louisiana. Defeat brought still other Southern generals into the church. While on the retreat toward

Atlanta, General Polk laid aside his sword long enough to baptize the wounded General Hood and the army commander Joseph E. Johnston.

A great portion of the plain folk of the South were deeply religious. They gave thanks to God for victories in the field and turned to him for solace in defeat and sorrow. On nine occasions the Confederate government set apart a day for fasting and praying in order to secure the blessing of God upon Southern arms and to lift the spirit of the hard-pressed people. Entire congregations assembled to pray for Confederate armies in combat; Congress acknowledged the hand of the Lord in Southern successes. Though a minister's appeal went unheeded that all Southerners pray at the same moment each day for victory, numerous churches kept their doors open and daily prayer meetings were held in many communities. Scores of thousands of soldiers and civilians were converted to the various faiths as religious revivals swept camp and countryside after Confederate reverses late in the conflict. Governor Pickens of South Carolina spoke for a host of Southerners when he said, "They have made it a holy war."

Religion was a powerful stimulant to Southern morale. Mrs. Mary Boykin Chesnut wrote after listening to the exhortations of Benjamin M. Palmer: "What a sermon! The preacher stirred my blood. My very flesh crept and tingled. A red-hot glow of patriotism passed through me. Such a sermon must strengthen the hearts and hands of many people." Soldiers often went to war with these sermons ringing in their ears. Missionaries and local ministers visited the camps to reinforce the efforts of chaplains in instilling both Christian piety and a zeal for combat among the troops. Bibles were distributed throughout the armies, along with countless soul-searing tracts entitled *A*

A Beleaguered People

Mother's Parting Words to Her Soldier Boy, Are You Ready To Die, Come to Jesus, and *You Are Soon To Be Damned.* Southern churchmen supported the Davis administration, urging the people to accept its unpopular but necessary measures for waging the war. Near the end of the struggle a Confederate congressman truly said: "The clergy have done more for the success of our cause than any other class. They have kept up the spirits of our people, have led in every philanthropic movement. . . . Not even the bayonets have done more."

In the end these efforts were made in vain. Southern prayers for divine succor went unanswered; the invaders silenced rebellious preachers, seized church property, and sometimes destroyed or desecrated houses of worship; churches fell idle and religious apathy spread in areas overrun by the enemy; faith in victory waned; and the South went down in defeat. Professor Coulter has written that the Confederacy might well have been victorious if it had been able to convert the war into a crusade in the name of religion. Notwithstanding what might have been, religion did in fact help to nerve the Southern people for the waging of a mighty war.

Southern educational resources served the war effort in various ways, though Confederate authorities attempted no systematic employment of them. Teachers who remained in the classroom provided intellectual support for Southern independence; college and university instructors often turned their knowledge to the development of weapons and munitions for the Confederacy. As an officer in the Ordnance Department, Professor John W. Mallet of the University of Alabama invented a superior artillery shell and capably managed the production of chemicals used in the manufacture of explosives. John and Joseph LeConte, brilliant scientists of South Carolina

College and the University of Georgia, held important positions in the Confederate Niter and Mining Bureau.

Southern schools were soon stricken. A number of educators in the ante-bellum South were men of Northern birth and sympathy who resigned their positions and left the region at the coming of secession. The most accomplished scholar in the group, Frederick A. P. Barnard, in 1861 left the presidency of the University of Mississippi and later took over Columbia College in New York City. President William T. Sherman of the Louisiana State Seminary and Military Academy went into the Union army to become the nemesis of the South.

The South had customarily imported her textbooks from the North. Now Southern writers and publishers set about to supply the region's need. A Confederate substitute for Noah Webster's famed blue-back speller was soon in print; Southern editions of *Caesar's Gallic War* came out; William Bingham of the Bingham School in North Carolina produced a serviceable Latin grammar. Various readers, geographies, and arithmetics appeared. Patterned after Northern textbooks in format and composition, the Southern publications suffered from want of good paper and experienced writing and editing. School books of the North and South differed chiefly in sentiment. Those of the North extolled American nationalism and deprecated slavery; those of the South praised Confederate valor and upheld the "peculiar institution." *Johnson's Elementary Arithmetic* contained this and other such problems: "If one Confederate soldier can whip 7 Yankees, how many soldiers can whip 49 Yankees?" *The Geographical Reader for Dixie Children*, by M. B. Moore, described the South as a Christian land of kind masters and contented Negro slaves. Confederate educators followed the American tradition of turning the three R's to the service of patriotism and citizenship.

Many Southern teachers and virtually all college students either volunteered or were conscripted into the army. University officials pled that their students be exempt from military service, but ultimately the petition was denied. Even had it been granted, the excitement of the times would have consumed all scholarly interests. "I cannot study," wrote a Mississippi youth, "and I wish to join a Horse Company." Most institutions of higher learning closed their doors before the war was over; those that remained open were reduced to token operation only. The state universities of Mississippi, Georgia, and South Carolina, the Louisiana State Seminary and Military Academy, and the College of Charleston ceased to function; in the entire state of Mississippi only one college, a denominational school, kept going. Some school property was destroyed by Northern soldiers. Buildings that were spared deteriorated woefully from neglect.

Although untouched by conscription, the South's primary and secondary schools were grievously crippled by the conflict. Many of her three thousand private high school academies fell idle for want of funds, as did many of the public schools. In communities where these institutions were kept open, terms of instruction often were drastically shortened and enrolments were slender. The women and old men who replaced departed teachers seldom were qualified for the task. Largely through the efforts of a dedicated Superintendent of Schools, Calvin Wiley, North Carolina alone among the Confederate states was able to salvage a state public school system out of the holocaust. Southern education was a major casualty of the war.

The Confederacy

Social life in the South was altered and in the end sadly blighted by the struggle, but popular diversions persisted in both victory and defeat. Plantation communities felt keenly the loss of their young men to the armies, but enough of them remained at home or returned on furlough from time to time to keep alive the embers of social amenity. Music and dancing still went on occasionally in the white-columned mansions, and thoroughbreds still ran on plantation racetracks. Traditional holidays continued to be observed in traditional ways; Christmas with eggnog parties and Santa Claus, and the Fourth of July with festivities and patriotic oratory of a Southern cast. Birthdays still brought forth the customary dinners, wines, gifts, and well-wishing. Hastened by war, marriages as always were occasions for dining and merrymaking. As the war progressed, food and drink diminished in quality and quantity, and clothing grew outmoded and shabby. But play went on among plantation folk even as the grim days came upon the Confederacy.

Except for the extreme youth of most of the boys who were still at home, wartime diversion among Southern farm families differed little from that before the war. Square dancing and singing remained favorite modes of entertainment. Summer religious revivals still gave opportunity for courting as well as moral regeneration. Picnics and barbecues were held, with cider and corn liquor as added refreshment; at corn huskings, quilting parties, and spinning bees work was blended with play; and hunting and fishing provided pleasure and food alike. Folk amusements enabled the plain people of the Confederacy to bear more easily the trials of war.

Social activities in the larger cities of the Confederacy were enlivened by the war. Richmond was the social as well as the political and military capital of the land. The city's population was more than three times as great as before the war, and her streets teemed with politicians, military officers, government clerks, laborers, refugees, job-seekers, soldiers on furlough, gamblers, confidence men, prostitutes, and the families of soldiers at the front and in the various hospitals. There were amusements to suit all tastes. With the pace being set by such vivacious ladies as Mrs. Varina Howell Davis, Mrs. Mary Boykin Chesnut, and the famed Baltimore belles, Constance and Hettie Cary, the socially elite lived in a whirl of receptions, parties, balls, dinners, home theatricals, and *matinées musicales*. The presence of leading Confederate statesmen and soldiers added an air of importance and gallantry to these affairs. For months during the summer of 1863 the youthful General John Bell Hood, desperately wounded at Gettysburg, was lionized by Richmond society. Gaiety persisted among this group even in the straitened latter months of the Confederacy. Those who owned plantations untouched by the armies, or whose friends and relatives owned such, from time to time brought provisions into the city for festive events. When food and drink were unavailable, "starvation parties" were given, with only water being served. Gambling halls and brothels in abundance catered to persons of cruder appetite. The masses of the city were able on rare occasions such as Christmas to enjoy a good meal, some of them even a turkey, and their children still shot a few firecrackers on this day. But life for them was generally too stringent for festivities. Instead, these people usually had to be content with neighborly visits and with attending religious revivals, open-air band concerts, and military reviews, which cost them nothing.

In the interior of the Confederacy the Negro slaves went

obediently about their tasks, though with less than usual efficiency on places where no white men remained to supervise. For these slaves life was little changed by the conflict, and much of the productivity of the South at war came from their hands. Fearing insurrection, local authorities early in the war made slave codes tighter and established special patrols and home guards to keep order among the Negroes. These measures doubtless encouraged the decorum that generally prevailed on the plantations. But most of the slaves either were reasonably content with their lot or were patient enough to wait for freedom to be conferred upon them by Northern invaders. Many slaves held a genuine affection for masters and their families. Lincoln's emancipation proclamation in January, 1863, had no immediate effect upon slaves behind the Southern lines. Even upon the approach of liberating Union armies, the Negroes showed no inclination to resort to mass violence. On these occasions the slaves left their masters by tens of thousands and flocked about the Northern encampments in a great jubilee of freedom; sometimes they became insolent and threatening toward Southern whites, and there were instances of violence. The exuberant blacks often pillaged, especially on estates abandoned by their owners, for the Negroes believed that the Lord had authorized a latter-day "spoiling of the Egyptians." In 1865 Mrs. Mary Boykin Chesnut wrote from South Carolina, "The fidelity of the Negroes is the principal topic everywhere. There seems not a single case of a Negro who betrayed his master; and yet they showed a natural and exultant joy at being free." Scholars have demonstrated that such statements of Negro loyalty were exaggerated. Nevertheless, through the vicissitudes of war, invasion, and emancipation the South was spared the horrors of Santo Domingo.

A Beleaguered People

Though the Confederacy produced no Joan of Arc leading armies to triumph in the field, the women of the South upheld the Southern cause with unsurpassed fervor. They expounded the righteousness of the war for Southern independence and affirmed the superior valor of Southern soldiers. They encouraged young men to rally to the Confederate colors and shamed the hesitant into enlisting. They vowed that the South would never be conquered, saying that if all her sons should fall, then her daughters would take up arms and expel the foe. A few Southern Amazons actually fought in the Confederate army, disguised as men. Foreign observers and Northern soldiers invading the South were agreed that her women were even more militant of spirit than her men. After ruling over the people of south Louisiana for many months, General Nathaniel P. Banks, commander of the Federal occupation forces, was convinced that Southern women had caused the war and that it was kept going through their encouragement.

Women supported the Confederacy in sundry ways. Their greatest contribution was in managing plantations and working farms while their husbands and sons were away in the armies. But women also served in every other capacity tolerated by the prevailing notions of feminine propriety. They sewed uniforms for the Quartermaster Department and made cartridges for the Ordnance Department. They filled various clerical positions in the government bureaus in Richmond. They taught school, made clothing, baked bread, and took over a great variety of other tasks commonly performed by men.

The most glamorous service done by women for the Confederacy was that of espionage. Scores of Southern women at one time or another gave to Confederate commanders important information on the military plans of the enemy. The

The Confederacy

most noted feminine spies were Belle Boyd and Mrs. Rose O'Neal Greenhow. Belle was a girl of seventeen at the outbreak of the war, living in Martinsburg in the Shenandoah Valley of Virginia. Repeatedly this bold young Rebel came through the lines bringing intelligence of Northern troop movements and dispositions; repeatedly she was imprisoned by the Federals, only to be released for want of evidence. Romance finally dulled her sense of Confederate patriotism, and late in the war she went to London where she was married to an officer of the Union navy. Mrs. Greenhow was a widow of social prominence in Washington, D.C., when the war began. An implacable Southerner, she was credited with giving Confederate officers information that enabled them to win the battle of First Manassas. Imprisoned in Washington as a spy, she was later released and deported to Richmond. She was drowned in 1864 off the coast of North Carolina while running the blockade on an official mission for the Confederacy.

Among the truest of Confederate heroines were the women who ministered to the sick and wounded soldiers of the South. In the early months of the war, before a system of military hospitals could be established, great numbers of Southern women voluntarily served the multitudes of casualties from camp and battlefield. Many women took disabled fighting men into their homes and nursed them back to health. Others contributed their services in the makeshift hospitals set up in warehouses in Richmond and at various points near the lines. Still others gave food and supplies out of their own homes and scoured the countryside in search of additional provisions for the ailing campaigners. An outstanding example of courage and sacrifice was rendered by Mrs. Arthur F. Hopkins of

Virginia and Alabama. Twice wounded on the battlefield while tending disabled soldiers, Mrs. Hopkins was called by General Joseph E. Johnston, "The Angel of the South." Groups of Catholic nuns distinguished themselves for skill, bravery, and compassion in aiding and comforting the wounded on battlefields and in hospitals.

Women founded the first hospitals for soldiers and served heroically as matrons of Confederate army hospitals. For establishing hospitals and aid stations throughout the South, Ella King Newsom of Arkansas became known as the "Florence Nightingale of the Southern army." The most famous hospital matrons were Kate Cumming of Mobile, Phoebe Pember of the great Chimborazo Hospital in Richmond, and Louisa Susanna McCord, a daughter of the South Carolina statesman Langdon Cheves. An observing Englishwoman in the Confederacy truly said, "Heaven only knows what the soldiers of the South would have done without the exertions of the women in their behalf."

In spite of the fierce patriotism of most Southern women, their spirit gave way at last under the burden of war, and their demoralization did much to wreck the Confederacy. Letters of wives imploring their husbands to come home were perhaps the greatest cause of desertion from the Southern army. Though some of these appeals were inspired by selfishness, fear, or loneliness, most of them arose out of severe hardship coupled with a growing belief that all sacrifice was in vain, that the Confederacy could not win the war. Only a will of iron could have withstood such a letter as this, written by a distraught woman to her husband in the ranks: "Before God, Edward, unless you come home we must die! Last night I was aroused by little Eddie's crying. . . . He said 'Oh, mamma,

The Confederacy

I'm so hungry!' And Lucy, Edward, your darling Lucy, she never complains, but she is growing thinner and thinner every day." By 1864 the armies were being showered by letters of this mood. The cries of her women heralded the defeat of the South.

Life in the Confederacy was at first gay and hopeful, and then it was filled with tribulation. Most of her people endured great loneliness, anxiety, and physical want, and many of them experienced the trials of enemy invasion. All suffered the loss of loved ones or friends among the host of war casualties. Early enthusiasm for the Southern cause gradually gave way to widespread apathy and defeatism as the people wearied of fighting and lost faith in victory. Absorbed in waging war, the Confederate government lacked the resources, the authority, and perhaps the desire to minister to the needs of the civilian population. Only in delivering mail did the Confederacy directly serve the people, and this became ever slower and less predictable as the transportation facilities of the South wore out. Most citizens of the Confederacy knew their central government solely through its conscription officers, provost marshals, impressment agents, and tax gatherers. These functionaries inspired no love for the Richmond authorities. Loyalty and affection for state and local community continued to hold highest claim on the emotions of many Southerners. Nevertheless, the Confederacy was supported by all manner of Southern resources through four years of unsurpassed travail.

X

Death of the Confederacy

News of the loss of Atlanta fell upon the Confederacy like a sentence of doom. Defeat was on every face and tongue. "There is no hope," wrote Mrs. Mary Boykin Chesnut; the famed theologian and exhorter to secession, Benjamin Morgan Palmer, prayed the prayer of desperation, "Help us oh God. Vain is the help of man." Overcome with frustration, the men of the South heaped even heavier abuse upon the leaders of the Confederacy. Those who two months earlier had chafed at Johnston's strategy of caution and called for a commander of bolder spirit now denounced Hood's rashness and cursed the President for making the change. Serene in the midst of Richmond's agitation, Lee came up from the lines of Petersburg to review with Davis and his cabinet the somber plight of the South.

The most urgent problem at the moment was that of Georgia, where Sherman was driving the inhabitants of Atlanta from their homes as he cleared his lines of communication in readiness for continued invasion. Enraged at the failure of Confederate authorities to save Atlanta and terrified over the fate that lay in store for the rest of his state, Governor Brown threatened to recall all Georgia troops from the Confederate army and use them in the protection of their native ground. Fearing that Hood would march the Georgia militia out of the state, Brown in his madness granted all its members a thirty-day furlough, thus further thinning the ranks of his only defenders. All the while he stormed and cried to Richmond for reinforcements.

Davis was powerless to send aid from Virginia, for Grant was at Lee's throat and not a soldier could be spared from the defense of the capital. Instead, the President made a frantic effort to strengthen Hood's army from other sources. Wounded soldiers able to travel were ordered back to their commands, and farmers and factory laborers detailed from military service were called to the colors, except for certain skilled artisans, armaments experts, and scientists actually indispensable for the maintenance and supply of the armies. Such measures were in vain; they only weakened the industries of the South and did not significantly strengthen her military forces.

In late September Davis left Richmond to go to Georgia. He wished to confer with Hood over future plans for the reduced Army of Tennessee; he was resolved to appeal directly to the people of Georgia and all the lower South for renewed faith in the Confederacy and redoubled effort against the foe. At Palmetto, Georgia, Davis met with Hood and approved his plan to move north into Tennessee in the hope of drawing Sherman after him. Addressing the troops of the ill-starred western army, Davis fired their hearts by disclosing their destination.

Death of the Confederacy

As Davis returned to Richmond he stopped frequently to speak in cities along the way. These addresses revealed in him a new awareness of the importance of gaining contact with the people and a new gift for doing so. At Macon, Georgia, he spoke with moving eloquence, saying, "Our cause is not lost. Sherman cannot keep up his long line of communication; and retreat sooner or later he must. And when that day comes, the fate that befell the army of the French Empire in its retreat from Moscow will be reenacted." Before a great rally at Augusta, Georgia, Davis urged Governor Brown and all of the men of Georgia and the South to throw themselves with re-kindled devotion into the struggle for constitutional government and freedom from Northern despotism. "This Confederacy," he declared, "is not played out as the croakers tell you. Let every man able to bear arms go to the front and the others must work at home for the cause. Our states must lean one upon the other; he who fights now for Georgia fights for all. We must beat Sherman and regain the line of the Ohio. Let men not ask what the law requires, but give whatever freedom demands."

Forces more powerful than Davis' oratory were at work on the emotions of his people. On November 4, as Hood moved toward Tennessee and Sherman stood poised for his epic march to the sea, the presidential election was held in the North. Then it became clear that the capture of Atlanta had taken effect, lifting the morale of the Northern people as it had depressed the spirit of the South. A perceptive scholar has said that this victory was the heaviest ballot cast in the election. Convinced now that Lincoln could win the war, the voters gave him a secure majority at the polls, and the peace movement in the North collapsed. This was the final blow to the Southern will to resist, for it gave proof of renewed determination in the North to press the war to victory.

Economic chaos spread rapidly over the South as hope of success vanished. Inflation and speculation quickened. Confederate finance had not responded to the remedies of the previous winter, and Secretary Memminger had been under scathing attack from Congress and the press. Representative Foote attempted unsuccessfully in May to force Memminger's removal; the Richmond *Examiner* wrote that the Secretary left undone all that ought to be done and did all that ought not be done. In June the dispirited Memminger resigned, though Davis besought him to remain. Davis then appointed the prominent Charleston merchant George A. Trenholm to the post.

A change in men at this late hour could not halt the plunge into bankruptcy. The commissioner of taxes reported in October that the taxes enacted earlier in the year had yielded somewhat less than $119,000,000—a pittance in comparison with the need. Efforts were futile to float the bond issue authorized the preceding winter, for there was little faith in the ability of the Confederacy to meet obligations years in the future. Only one-fourth of these bonds were ever sold, and the purchases doubtless were made simply out of a spirit of patriotic sacrifice. Compulsory funding failed to reduce the vast amount of paper currency and raise its value. A momentary drop in prices came when the funding began, but inflation soon resumed its course, and ultimately the attempt was abandoned. Old notes continued to circulate side by side with the new, and by the end of the year neither was worth more than two cents on the dollar in gold. In August a Richmond lady spent $1,500 in an hour of shopping. A paper of pins cost her $5; butter was $25 a pound, eggs $6 a dozen, milk $4 a quart, and cigars $10 apiece.

Ruins left by war in Columbia, South Carolina.
Photograph by G. N. Barnard, 1865

Richmond in ruins. View taken from south side of Canal Basin, showing Capitol and Custom House, Richmond, Virginia, April, 1865

Richmond in ruins. View of part of the "Burnt District," Richmond, Virginia, April, 1865

Death of the Confederacy

Secretary Trenholm was perhaps the wealthiest man in the Confederacy and was regarded as a financial genius by the people of the South. His appointment was widely applauded, even by the congressional opposition and the anti-Davis press. Trenholm strove heroically to rescue the Confederacy from economic ruin by curbing the issue of treasury notes, taxing heavily, pleading with the citizens to purchase Confederate bonds, and shipping cotton overseas in order to secure foreign credit. But the Congress that hailed his nomination refused to support his stern program for recovery. In November, 1864, he recommended a continuation of the tax in kind after the war, and in order to reduce the currency he urged that planters and farmers be permitted to pay this postwar tax at once and at the inflated prices then prevailing. Trenholm also called for additional taxes and bonds sufficient to raise $360,000,000 for the expenses of the government. Congress rejected these and all other drastic tax proposals and instead turned back to the printing of additional currency.

In the last days of the Confederacy, Trenholm called upon the people for direct donations; like the ancient Hebrews who gave their treasure for the building of the temple, many patriotic Southerners sacrificed the very last of their most precious belongings in food, heirlooms, watches, jewelry, and gold. Trenholm himself gave $200,000. All was futile. Paper currency of baffling variety swirled through the South's markets, competing for her dwindling commodities and tempting the people to further excesses of speculation. Besides immense quantities of Confederate notes, there were issues of notes by states, banks, and insurance and railroad companies. The value of all sank steadily as the shadows lengthened over the Confederacy. Soon all were worthless.

The Confederacy

The Confederate home front now gave way. A sweeping conviction that the cause was lost was coupled with indescribable suffering among the masses of the people to bring on this debacle. Social disintegration spread through the remote hill and piney woods country where Confederate authority had never been strong. Officers of the law were defied with impunity, and marauding gangs preyed upon the families of men away at the front. A woman wrote from western Louisiana, "Lawless men have been permitted to band themselves together, and roam at will, . . . insulting, chastising, robbing, burning houses, murdering the families of our soldiers; and in some instances despoiling in the most brutal manner, wives, daughters and sisters of that which is dearer than life itself— their honor." Smouldering mountain feuds burst into open warfare as old hatreds among the clans were fanned by opposing sectional loyalties. Wives and parents besought husbands and sons to withdraw from a hopeless and iniquitous struggle, from a "rich man's war and a poor man's fight." Desertion became epidemic and the armies melted away as from the plague. Distraught by the anguished appeals of countless women to have their men exempted from conscription, a young official of the Confederate War Department wrote with melancholy truth, "The iron is gone deep into the heart of society."

Still the war went on. Davis and his advisers continued to search desperately for measures that would strengthen the failing arm of the South, and a heroic minority of civilians and soldiers was as indomitable now as in the beginning. Grant pressed relentlessly upon Lee's thin lines at Petersburg, confident that time and winter were allies of the Union—that cold, disease, hunger, and hopelessness were eating away the Army of Northern Virginia more certainly than were Northern shells. From time to time the Federal commander hurled his great army against the Southern position, hoping to break through and deliver the coup de grâce to the mortally wounded Confederacy. Meanwhile, Sheridan's army moved up the Shenandoah Valley, spreading destruction and stripping the land of sustenance. Sheridan faithfully carried out Grant's wish that the area be left so bare that "crows flying over it . . . [would] have to carry their provender with them."

As Grant strained at the jugular of the Confederacy, Sherman laid open its body. Sending a portion of his army under General John M. Schofield to reinforce General George H. Thomas in Tennessee against the threat of Hood, Sherman launched his historic punitive expedition through the exposed regions of the lower South. On November 16 his army of 60,000 veterans marched out of the smouldering ruins of Atlanta, singing "John Brown's body lies a-mouldering in the grave." For more than a month this force was lost to the outside world as it moved virtually unopposed toward the sea, living off the fat of the land. Sherman left a broad wake of desolation, of burned towns and villages, plundered homes, fields, and pastures, twisted rails, and occasional murdered citizens and ravished women. On December 21 he took Savannah on the coast.

Meantime, Hood led his army to its destruction. His strategy was bold and imaginative; it contemplated the annihilation of the various scattered Union forces in Tennessee before they could be united by Thomas at Nashville. But the execution of the plan was abominable. Seized by some unexplained lethargy, Hood on November 29 permitted Schofield's corps to escape a well-laid trap at Spring Hill, Tennessee, and the following day Hood sacrificed the heart of his army in a suicidal assault upon Schofield's earthworks at Franklin. Schofield then joined Thomas in Nashville, and Hood fatuously laid siege to the Union army there that was now more than twice the size of his own. Disregarding Grant's insistent orders to attack immediately, Thomas methodically completed his concentration and awaited favorable weather. On December 15–16 he struck and shattered the Confederate army in the decisive battle of Nashville, then pursued its fragments relentlessly until they found refuge beyond the Tennessee River in Alabama. The Army of Tennessee was an army no more.

From the Appalachians to the Mississippi there was now no Confederate force capable of more than harassing Federal garrisons and communications. East of the Appalachians there was only Lee's army, and it endured solely as a symbol of devotion to its peerless chief, for every vestige of hope was gone. On February 1 Sherman marched out of Savannah toward an ultimate junction with Grant in Virginia. Sherman's army swept through South Carolina like an avenging flame; every soldier considered himself an instrument for venting the wrath of the nation upon the mother of secession. The depredations of the march to the sea were re-enacted in fuller measure; South Carolina's most venerable plantation mansions were wantonly destroyed; and on February 17 Columbia, the state capital, was put to the torch, though Sherman denied responsibility for it.

Hood's disaster in Tennessee and the sweep of Sherman's army through the lower South destroyed what small residue of confidence the administration had been able to salvage from earlier defeats in the field and conflicts of authority within the Confederacy. From every quarter arose the voices of censure and accusation. Stephens returned to Richmond and poured forth his venom before the Senate, arraigning the government for incompetence and despotism. Congress now succumbed to the disease of state rights, though during most of the war this otherwise weak and imperfect body had been moved primarily by the spirit of Southern nationalism. Impressment was repudiated and all supplies required to be purchased in the open market; restrictions on blockade-running were abandoned and the government left without the means of importing arms and other necessities for the destitute armies; and the lawmakers refused to suspend anew the writ of habeas corpus, though Davis pled that it be done, saying, "[It] is not simply expedient, but almost indispensable to the successful conduct of the war." Congress no longer represented a nation, but instead a league of "sovereign states."

A movement now arose in Congress to depose Davis and replace him with Lee, and the hostile press called for Lee to be made dictator in the manner of ancient Rome. Describing the government as "a pandemonium of imbecility, laxity, weakness, failure," the Charleston *Mercury* demanded, "Cannot Lee be raised to Executive power at Richmond?" General Longstreet had once suggested this to Lee, who had ignored it; according to an account given after the war, such a proposal was at this time made to Lee by an emissary of Congress, only to meet with categorical refusal. Biographer Douglas Southall Freeman says that the records fail to show that Congress ever made this overture. Had it been made, it unquestionably would have been rejected, for Lee's nature precluded the role of Napoleon.

Unable to establish Lee as dictator, Congress instead created for him the position of General in Chief of the armies. A year earlier this could have been of great consequence, since it would have given to the Southern military effort a vitally needed unity of command, and would have placed at the helm the one man capable of rekindling the confidence of the people. But the Confederacy was now beyond salvation. Moreover, the position was created under circumstances that robbed it of effectiveness. It represented a vote of no confidence in Davis' leadership, and for this reason his staunchest supporters in Congress opposed it. Mrs. Davis is supposed to have said of the act, "If I were he [Davis] I would die or be hung before I would submit to the humiliation." Nevertheless, Davis signed the unpalatable act and immediately named Lee to the post. Lee accepted the title, but in doing so he deliberately rebuked those who regarded it as a symbol of censure against Davis. Lee said, "I am indebted alone to the kindness of his Excellency, the President, for my nomination to this high and arduous office." These were the words of a reluctant generalissimo, who by now was almost without armies to command.

The crushing defeats of the fall and winter revived the Southern peace movement and added many converts. In October Representative William W. Boyce of South Carolina openly indorsed Vice President Stephens' visionary peace plan and urged in Congress the calling of a convention, North and South, to end the war. Boyce hoped to influence the voters of the North to elect McClellan President and thus pave the way to a negotiated peace. It perhaps would have been astute for Davis to support this strategy. One historian has suggested that a Machiavellian peace overture by Davis at this time possibly could have unseated Lincoln in the election, thereby restoring Southern morale and sowing doubt and confusion among the Northern people. But Davis would have none of it and Boyce's appeal was lost. Attempts were made later by other Southern

Death of the Confederacy

congressmen to call a peace conference, and in January, 1865, Stephens again took up the cry. Davis was convinced that peace could come in one of two ways only: either by winning the war and achieving Southern independence, or by losing the war and returning to the Union on Northern terms. He was suddenly presented with an opportunity to permit Stephens himself to test this proposition.

At this time the aged Union editor and politician Francis P. Blair arrived in Richmond. He had hit upon a scheme which he thought would bring the warring sections of the nation together again. Let North and South make an armistice, he urged, and together drive out the French forces then violating the soil of Mexico and defying the Monroe Doctrine of the United States. Lincoln had permitted Blair to come south through the lines to present his idea to the Confederate authorities. Davis had little interest in the proposed Mexican venture, but he agreed to a meeting of leaders, North and South, to discuss the matter. If for any purpose an armistice could be arranged, he reasoned, Southern independence would probably be assured, for the war could then be resumed only with extreme difficulty. The result was the famous Hampton Roads Conference of February 3, 1865, between Lincoln and Seward on the one side and a Confederate commission of Stephens, former Associate Justice of the United States Supreme Court John A. Campbell, and Confederate Senator R. M. T. Hunter on the other. Nothing came of the meeting. Though expressing hope of a "spirit of sincere liberality" in dealing with the seceded states, Lincoln was adamant in his demand that the South return to her old allegiance. In his instructions to the Confederate commissioners, Davis was just as firm in his insistence upon Southern independence. Failure to achieve a negotiated peace enabled him to turn to his people with the two alternatives—independence or submission.

Impending ruin made of Davis what he had not been before—an inspiring war leader. Armed with Lincoln's refusal to consider any terms of peace save submission, Davis appealed to his people in the one great impassioned oration of his presidential career. It was done on the evening of February 6 before a mass meeting at the African Church in Richmond. Snow lay thick upon the ground, and the pallid and worn appearance of the President excited the sympathy of all hearers. Davis' message came straight from the heart, free of tedious legalism and constitutional dialectic. For a moment it stirred into life the dying embers of Southern resistance. He expressed regret that he was not addressing a victory celebration, but he was thankful that there were still citizens willing to lay all they had upon the altar of their country. Lincoln had invited a peace conference, Davis said, only to reject all honorable overtures, and now the war must go on. Let the absent soldiers of the South return to their regiments, cried Davis, and the Confederacy would be free within the year. "Let us then unite our hands and hearts, lock our shields together and we may well believe that before another summer solstice falls upon us, it will be the enemy who will be asking us for conferences and occasions in which to make known our demands."

With these bold, sincere words Davis imparted to his listeners a measure of his own courage and conviction. Even his bitterest critics were affected. Pollard of the *Examiner* later wrote that never before had he been so moved by the power of as many words; and Stephens said that the address was "bold, undaunted and confident." Benjamin and others made similar appeals in Richmond, while supporters of the administration bore messages of inspiration throughout the South.

As the lifeblood of the Confederacy ran swiftly out, Davis and his counselors turned in desperation to the most revolutionary of all measures for sustaining their stricken cause—the employment of Negro slaves as soldiers, to be followed by emancipation at the end of the war. Confederate leaders caught two glimmers of hope in this proposed line of action. By arming the slaves the South could replenish her shattered armies, and by emancipating them she could remove perhaps the real obstacle to foreign recognition and intervention. This would be the Confederate riposte—moral, military, and diplomatic—to Lincoln's emancipation proclamation.

The idea of using Negro troops in the Southern army was not new. It was conceived early in the war by General Patrick Cleburne and other officers of the Army of Tennessee, and after the loss of Chattanooga in the autumn of 1863 Cleburne had circulated a statement among his fellow officers advocating the employment of Negro soldiers. The recommendation was voted down, and at Davis' order word of the affair was suppressed for fear of spreading demoralization and dissent among the people. The thought did not die, but lay dormant awaiting to be rekindled by despair.

The fall of Atlanta and the dwindling of the armies thereafter brought Davis a step nearer to the enrolment of Negro soldiers. In November of 1864 he asked Congress for authority to purchase slaves to be employed as cooks and teamsters in order to free more troops for combat. The Negroes were to be emancipated at the end of the war in return for faithful service. Secretary Seddon went farther at this time and recommended using

Negroes as full-fledged soldiers. Voices of opposition were immediately lifted. The ailing Rhett wrote a letter filled with indignation that the Confederate government should assume the power to emancipate slaves, and Congress fumed and debated and bridled away from a question so charged with emotion.

Governor William Smith of Virginia then took the initiative, urging his state legislature to arm the Negroes and thus avoid disaster. And on January 11, 1865, in reply to an inquiry by a Virginia lawmaker, General Lee wrote his famous letter on the use of slaves as soldiers. With unassailable logic Lee pointed to the likelihood of Federal victory, to be achieved in part by the use of Southern Negroes, and certainly to be followed by emancipation. Let the state governments forestall this, he said, by arming their slaves against the foe, and let the loyalty and courage of the Negroes be secured by the promise of emancipation once Southern independence were achieved. Bitter as this course might be, he reasoned, it was infinitely preferable to subjugation and forced emancipation.

Davis now turned his support to a bill in Congress for arming and ultimately freeing the Negroes, and in late February he wrote, "It is now becoming daily more evident to all reflecting persons that we are reduced to choosing whether the negroes shall fight for or against us, and that all arguments as to the positive advantages or disadvantages of employing them are beside the question." Angry debate crackled in Congress and throughout the South over the issue. Wigfall and Hunter in the Senate and Foote in the House led the opposition, with Hill in the Senate and Barksdale in the House upholding the measure out of stark military necessity. The great organs of vituperation, the *Examiner* and the *Mercury*, were unsparing in their denunciation, and even as staunch a supporter of the administration as General Howell Cobb attacked the plan as the "most pernicious idea that had been suggested since the war began." Congress finally authorized the use of Negro troops but refused to provide for emancipation. The few Negroes enrolled in the Confederate army were never sent into combat.

Confederate leaders in these last days cherished the forlorn hope of gaining recognition and aid from England and France by freeing the slaves. There was a certain logic behind this feeling. Early in the war Yancey had noted the deep hostility of the English people toward slavery, and Mason and Slidell were embarrassed by this antipathy both in England and France. The perceptive Hotze had written:

It is the great peculiarity of England that the heart of the country is thoroughly religious. . . . To this very hour the great mass of the people have no other terms to express the nature of the [American] conflict. The emancipation of the Negro from the slavery of Mrs. Beecher Stowe's heroes is the one idea of the millions of British who know no better and do not care to know.

Davis and Benjamin came tardily to the view that slavery was perhaps the principal obstacle to recognition, and now, with the Confederacy in shambles, they decided upon a move to eliminate the obstacle.

In February, 1865, Duncan Kenner of Louisiana was dispatched to Europe to make the overture. Kenner sailed in disguise from New York and joined Mason and Slidell in Paris. When Kenner disclosed the nature of his mission, Mason was aghast and said at first that he would have none of it. But seeing finally that he must, Mason agreed to return to London for a last effort to sway the British government from its course. Slidell was to make a like attempt before the Emperor.

The Confederacy

These were overtures born of despair and they came to naught. Napoleon uttered his customary platitudes of sympathy for the South; but he repeated his determination not to move alone, and he truthfully said that the issue of slavery had never governed his policy toward the Confederacy. On March 14 Mason was admitted to an interview with Prime Minister Palmerston. Oddly the Southern emissary did not explicitly offer emancipation in return for recognition, but he made hints to this effect that he thought were unmistakable. Like Napoleon, the British statesman spoke warmly of the Southern cause, but refused to yield his position. England could not risk recognition, he said, because the Confederacy had as yet failed to establish her independence beyond all reasonable hazard. The last hope of European intervention was gone.

The end of the Confederacy came on swiftly after the failure in early 1865 to negotiate peace or gain foreign recognition and aid. Davis' powerful appeal at the African Church touched the heartstrings of many of his people, but it could not restore morale to a land riven by invasion and bled white by four years of savage warfare. Sherman was now in North Carolina completing his mission of havoc and moving irresistibly toward junction with Grant in Virginia. Retreating impotently before him were the relics of all major Confederate forces east of the Mississippi River, except Lee's Army of Northern Virginia. Even the shadow of the Army of Tennessee was there after an incredible journey of almost one thousand miles by rail and foot from northern Mississippi. Commanding this aggregation of troops was Joseph E. Johnston, recalled to the field not by Davis but by General in Chief Robert E. Lee. Considering the means at hand, the Southern concentration was a masterpiece of skill and effort. But it was a work of futility, for Sherman's strength was too great to be denied. Late in March the invading Union army took Goldsboro in the center of the state, and there, supplied by rail from the recently captured port of Wilmington, Sherman settled down to await further orders from Grant.

Meantime, the final scenes in the tragedy of the Confederacy were being enacted in the capitol at Richmond and in the trenches of Petersburg. Congress virtually ceased to function after the futile and exhausting debate over the arming and emancipation of the slaves. Only a plea by Davis kept the lawmaking body in session beyond early March; it might as well have disbanded then, for nothing of significance came out of it. On the eighteenth Congress adjourned; its members departed for their homes, knowing well that they would assemble no more. The President and his cabinet continued to ponder the plight of the Confederacy, but most of them were aware that it was now settled. Secretary of War John C. Breckinridge, who had succeeded Seddon a month earlier, daily sat idle in his office awaiting the inevitable end. The only men in Richmond who steadfastly refused to admit defeat were the haggard Davis and the blandly imperturbable Benjamin.

It is impossible to say just when Robert E. Lee first knew that the Army of Northern Virginia was doomed, but the realization must have come to him as he contemplated Sherman's unfaltering march through the Carolinas. The one remaining hope for the Confederacy lay in the remote possibility that Lee could join Johnston and destroy first Sherman and then Grant before the Union armies could be united. This could be done, if at all, only by abandoning Richmond, but Davis stubbornly refused to give up the capital. He chose instead to risk all on the ability of Lee and his weary men to withstand indefinitely the crush of the iron ring that was being forged about them. Strategically this was folly, and Davis has been amply censured for insisting upon it. Yet considered from another point of view, it was not wholly without reason. Perhaps Confederate historian Robert Selph Henry is right in saying, "An established nation may lose its capital and live . . . but for a people in 'rebellion' to do so, would mean the end."

Thus Lee's army manned its lines as the month of March ran out. Davis and his cabinet continued to meet and go through the motions of discussing policy, publishing regulations, and rendering reports. One would have thought the Confederacy established beyond peradventure. Speculation went on unabated in the market places of Richmond, where Confederate notes were exchanged for gold at the rate of one hundred dollars for one, and flour sold for $1,500 a barrel and bacon for $20 a pound. A profound gloom came over the capital as the cannon fire grew in intensity about her and the realization spread that her days were numbered. Here and there a hysterical gaiety flared up amid the general sorrow, and lavish dinners were held by some even as Confederate heroes were being borne to the grave.

Richmond's last day was Sunday, April 2. The spring sky was incongruously fair for the somber events that lay in store for the city. Davis went as usual to worship in St. Paul's Episcopal Church, but he went with drawn face and heavy heart, because he knew at last that the hour of reckoning was at hand. Grant's assaults had for a week grown hourly more severe, and Lee's dispatches had become increasingly ominous. The final fateful message reached the President in his pew; the army faced immediate disaster and the lines could be held for only a few more hours. Richmond was lost. Davis heard the message

Destruction in Atlanta. Demolition of railroad
depot in Atlanta, Georgia

General Robert E. Lee. Photograph by Vannerson, 1864

A dead Confederate soldier in the trenches of Fort Mahone before Petersburg, Virginia, April 3, 1865

with an expression "as impenetrable as an iron mask," then he arose and walked out of the church. That night at eleven o'clock, as Richmond lay in mourning and her black-clad daughters wept openly in the streets, Davis and his cabinet left the city on a train going south. The "flight into oblivion" had begun.

That same night Lee abandoned the Petersburg trenches and marched west, hoping to reach the railroad to Danville and ultimately to join Johnston in North Carolina. The march was a nightmare of hunger, exhaustion, and despair. Grant pursued relentlessly, and the fleeing Confederates were harassed by Sheridan's cavalry on all sides. Only respect for its commander held the forlorn army together. In the words of the novelist Ellen Glasgow, "Lee was still somewhere to the front, so his army followed." But not all followed. Flesh and blood had limits, and the famished and dispirited troops left the ranks by battalions. Lee withdrew from Petersburg with 28,000 men; after a week of marching and fighting, fewer than half that number remained to "stack muskets at Appomattox." The retreat was made in vain. Grant's army outdistanced and enveloped the faltering Southern column, and by April 9 the route of escape was closed. Though many of the Confederates would have sacrificed themselves in a final suicidal attack upon the Union lines, Lee would not hear of it. Instead, he rode away to the village of Appomattox Court House. There in the most dramatic scene of American history the Virginia cavalier surrendered himself and his army to the magnanimous commoner who had overcome them.

The Confederacy's time had come; all that followed the fall of Richmond and the Great Surrender was pathetic anticlimax. Davis continued the flight south. His mind was hardened against the awareness of defeat, and he cherished the empty hope of stirring the Southern people to renewed effort. At Greensboro, North Carolina, he vainly urged General Johnston to carry on the war. Johnston wisely refused and on April 18 surrendered his little band to Sherman. Davis pressed on, dreaming of a revived Confederacy beyond the Mississippi, where General Kirby Smith still had an army in the field. On May 4 the remaining Confederate troops east of the Mississippi River were surrendered. Davis' visions of continued resistance were soon ended. On May 10 near the village of Irwinsville, Georgia, the President of the Confederacy became a prisoner of the United States. Sixteen days later General Kirby Smith surrendered the Trans-Mississippi Department.

The Confederacy was dead.

XI

In Retrospect

Almost a century has passed since Appomattox, and countless explanations have been offered for the fall of the Confederacy. People of the South have generally believed that the Confederacy was overwhelmed by weight of numbers. The generation of Northerners who fought the war was convinced that victory was the reward of superior virtue. Writing in the 1870's, the abolitionist Henry Wilson saw God's hand in the destruction of slavery and the Confederacy. Historian James Ford Rhodes thought that a telling reason for Northern triumph was the moral ascendancy of Abraham Lincoln over Jefferson Davis. Most scholars of the twentieth century have discredited the traditional reasoning of both North and South and have attributed the defeat of the Confederacy to internal defects and inept leadership. In 1919 Nathaniel W. Stephenson laid Southern failure to inner dissension and the Union blockade. Six years later Frank Owsley convincingly expounded the thesis that the seeds of death were sown at the birth of the Confederacy in the principle of state rights. American experience in World War II has enabled historians at mid-century to apply the concept of total war to their analysis of the Civil War. In this view, Lincoln, Grant, and Sherman emerge as practitioners of a comprehensive, superior military strategy; Lee becomes a great "old-fashioned" general, Grant and Sherman great "modern" generals. Today some students of the Confederacy suggest weaknesses even more fundamental than state rights, defective political administration, and archaic military strategy. The will of the South was palsied, they say, by a deep sense of guilt arising out of the sins of slavery and disunion.

Belief that the Confederacy was defeated because of her imperfections rests upon the premise that the South possessed sufficient resources to win the war if she had used them effectively. The inferior strength of the Confederacy is said to have been adequate for defense against the North. It is pointed out that the American Colonies achieved independence against greater odds in men and wealth than those facing the Southern people in their struggle for nationhood.

The Confederacy was afflicted with many weaknesses. Some were flaws common to all revolutionary movements and infant nations. Others were inherent in the nature of the South, thus supporting the dictum of the military philosopher Von Clausewitz that wars are fought according to the characteristics of the societies waging them. State rights, a primary element of the Confederacy, diffused much of her energy, and bitter personal feuds parted her leaders. Davis failed to adopt a fully co-ordinated military strategy or to name Lee general in chief until it was too late for effect. Agrarian hostility to taxation and distrust of government credit helped to prostrate Confederate finance and bring on inflation with the varied ills that came in its wake. Unionism dampened the war spirit of an indeterminable number of Southerners, and resentment among the poor over alleged favors to the rich spread doubt and demoralization. An individualistic folk of lingering frontier heritage chafed at the discipline required by modern war. A limited view of world affairs led Southern authorities into false diplomacy. The Confederacy did not make full use of her resources.

But the proposition that the South had enough resources to withstand a determined Northern assault is questionable, and comparison with the experience of the American Colonies is deceptive. Writing after the Napoleonic epoch, Von Clausewitz estimated that with a numerical superiority of 2.5 to 1 a western European alliance could conquer France. He did not presume an inferiority of French morality, will, social cohesion, political leadership, or military strategy. The Union held a numerical advantage of 2.5 to 1 over the Confederacy, counting Negro slaves in the Southern population; in military manpower and industrial strength the North was more heavily favored. British power during the American Revolution was never mobilized against the rebellious provinces to the extent that Northern strength was turned upon the South, and European allies decisively supported the American cause with money and armed forces. There is reason to believe that with all else equal the Confederacy lacked the physical assets for a successful war of independence. She could triumph only by exercising over the North sufficiently greater unity, skill, and will to compensate for the inadequacy of resources. In this she failed. For want of necessary strength, or of its equivalent in superior unity and skill, the Southern will declined and the

Confederacy fell. In this sense Professor Coulter is right in saying that the South lost the war because she "did not will hard enough and long enough to win."

Elaboration upon the Confederacy's weaknesses has often obscured her formidable strength. In proportion to population, industrial resources, and wealth, the Southern republic developed military power seldom if ever equalled in modern times. With 9,000,000 people, more than one-third of whom provided no soldiers, the Confederacy fought the "most harrowing" war of the century in the western world. In spite of shortcomings, Davis led the South with unfaltering devotion and courage. However old-fashioned, Lee and Jackson and other Confederate generals inspired their followers to unsurpassed feats on the battlefield. Southern armies reached a maximum strength in 1863 of about 260,000 troops present for duty. This was probably a larger portion of national population, even including slaves, than had ever before been placed in the field. Notwithstanding weaknesses in industry, finance, and transportation, the South maintained both soldiers and civilians largely with her own hands. Her resistance was so determined that it was overcome only after four years of prodigious strife and after immense regions of the Confederacy were laid waste through total war. Out of approximately 1,000,000 Southern men enrolled in the Confederate ranks during the conflict, more than one-fourth died of wounds and disease. Almost 100,000 were killed in battle. In relation to the number of Southern white people, these service casualties were as great as those endured by major European participants in the wars of the twentieth century. If the North during the Civil War had suffered commensurately she would have lost more than 1,000,000 men instead of 360,000. The American Colonies in revolt against

In Retrospect

England would have lost 94,000 men instead of 12,000. The United States in World War II would have lost well over 6,000,000 men instead of somewhat more than 300,000. The Confederacy rendered the heaviest sacrifice in lives and substance ever made by Americans.

The Confederacy was born of an authentic Southern urge for independence. She lived briefly and in bitter tribulation. The Confederacy was destroyed by an authentic Northern urge to retain the Union.

Important Dates

1860 Secession of South Carolina, December 20

1861 Secession of Mississippi, Florida, Alabama, Georgia, Louisiana, and Texas, January 9 to February 1
Provisional Government of Confederate States of America formed in Montgomery, February 8
Jefferson Davis and Alexander Stephens elected Provisional President and Vice President, February 9
Bombardment and capture of Fort Sumter, April 12–14
Lincoln's call for troops, April 15
Secession of Virginia, Arkansas, North Carolina, and Tennessee, April 17 to June 8
England recognizes Confederate belligerency, May 14
Battle of First Manassas, July 21
Confederate commissioners Mason and Slidell seized on British ship "Trent," November 8

1862 Permanent Confederate government inaugurated, February 22
Battle of Shiloh, April 6–7
Confederacy adopts conscription, April 16

Important Dates

Loss of New Orleans, May 1
McClellan repulsed before Richmond, June 26 to July 1
British government considers and refuses recognition of
   Confederate independence, September 14 to November 11
Battle of Sharpsburg, September 16–17

1863 Battle of Chancellorsville, May 1–4
   Battle of Gettysburg, July 1–3
   Loss of Vicksburg, July 4
   Trans-Mississippi Department becomes virtually autonomous,
      July 25
   Confederate commissioner withdrawn from England, August
      4
   Chickamauga-Chattanooga campaign, September 19 to No-
      vember 25

1864 Grant placed in command of all Union armies, March 9
   Opening of Grant's general offensive to crush the Confed-
      eracy, May 4
   Siege of Petersburg begins, June 15
   Struggle for Atlanta begins, July 6
   Fall of Atlanta, September 2
   Sherman marches to the sea, November 16 to December 13
   Battle of Nashville, December 15–16
   Fall of Savannah, December 21

1865 Hampton Roads Peace Conference, February 3
   Lee named general in chief of Confederate armies, February
      6
   Richmond and Petersburg abandoned, April 2
   Lee surrenders, April 9
   Joseph E. Johnston surrenders, April 26
   Capture of Jefferson Davis, May 10
   Trans-Mississippi Department surrenders, May 26

Suggested Readings

Literature on the Confederacy is vast and is still growing. Not only do new monographs and treatises on old themes appear in print almost weekly; new sources in the form of diaries, journals, and letters are constantly being brought to light and published. I make no attempt here to give a complete bibliography on the subject, but rather to present those books that have been most useful to me in the writing of this volume.

Greatest of all sources on the Confederacy is the monumental *The War of the Rebellion: A Compilation of the Official Records of the Union and Confederate Armies* (128 vols.; Washington, 1880–1901). The *Official Records* deal primarily with military policies and campaigns, but they also contain a wealth of information on virtually all aspects of life in the wartime South. Significant documents of Confederate history are compiled in J. D. Richardson (ed.), *Messages and Papers of the Confederacy* (2 vols.; Nashville, 1906); and *Journal of the Congress of the Confederate States of America* (8 vols.; Washington, 1904).

Among the most interesting and important of sources on the Confederacy are the diaries, journals, and memoirs of men and women who lived or traveled in the South during the Civil War. Some of the most revealing accounts of Southern life are in Mrs.

Suggested Readings

Mary Boykin Chesnut, *A Diary from Dixie* (new ed.; Cambridge, 1949), edited by Ben Ames Williams; Judith White McGuire, *Diary of a Southern Refugee* (New York, 1868); Sarah Morgan Dawson, *A Confederate Girl's Diary* (Boston and New York, 1913); *The Journal of Julia Le Grand* (Richmond, 1911), edited by Kate Mason Rowland and Mrs. Morris L. Croxall; and *Brockenburn: The Journal of Kate Stone, 1861–1868* (Baton Rouge, 1955), edited by John Q. Anderson. Exceedingly valuable insights into Confederate administration and affairs in Richmond are found in John B. Jones, *A Rebel War Clerk's Diary at the Confederate States Capital* (2 vols.; Philadelphia, 1866); and *Inside the Confederate Government: The Diary of Robert Garlick Hill Kean* (New York, 1957), edited by Edward Younger. Of some use is John H. Reagan, *Memoirs* (New York and Washington, 1906), edited by Walter F. McCaleb. The most significant descriptions of the embattled South by foreigners are in William Howard Russell, *My Diary North and South* (Boston, 1863); and Arthur J. L. Fremantle, *Three Months in the Southern States* (New York, 1864).

Histories of the Confederacy written by former Confederates are generally disappointing, yet useful. Jefferson Davis vindicated the Southern cause in *The Rise and Fall of the Confederate Government* (2 vols.; New York, 1881) and *A Short History of the Confederate States of America* (New York, 1890). Alexander Stephens expounded the constitutionality of secession and the Confederacy in *A Constitutional View of the Late War Between the States* (2 vols.; Philadelphia, 1868–70). Some insights into the nature of the Confederacy are provided in J. L. M. Curry, *Civil History of the Confederate States* (Richmond, 1900). Characteristically hostile to Davis and his supporters is the wartime editor Edward A. Pollard, *Southern History of the War* (2 vols.; New York, 1866) and *The Lost Cause* (New York, 1866). Other works by contemporary Southerners are John Minor Botts, *The Great Rebellion* (New York, 1866); and Henry S. Foote, *War of the Rebellion* (New York, 1866).

There is an abundance of secondary works on the Confederacy. Chapters in the following general histories of the United States are given to the subject: James Ford Rhodes, *History of the United States from the Compromise of 1850*, Vols. IV and V; and Edward Channing, *History of the United States*, Vol. VI.

The Confederacy

The Confederacy is thoroughly treated in James G. Randall, *The Civil War and Reconstruction* (New York and Boston, 1937). A commendably brief and highly readable work on the Confederacy is Nathaniel W. Stephenson, *The Day of the Confederacy* (New Haven, 1919). Robert S. Henry, *The Story of the Confederacy* (Indianapolis, 1931), is well written and accurate, with major emphasis on military policy and campaigns. The most exhaustive histories of the Confederacy, and ones upon which I have heavily relied, are E. Merton Coulter, *The Confederate States of America, 1861–1865* (Baton Rouge, 1950); and Clement Eaton, *A History of the Southern Confederacy* (New York, 1956). Professor Coulter touches only lightly on military campaigns but presents a great wealth of material on all other aspects of Confederate history. Professor Eaton provides a skilful blending of military and civil history. Vivid pictorial histories wholly or partially about the Confederacy are Lamont Buchanan, *A Pictorial History of the Confederacy* (New York, 1951); David Donald *et al* (eds.), *Divided We Fought* (New York, 1956); and Fletcher Pratt (ed.), *Civil War in Pictures* (New York, 1955). Various histories of the South devote chapters to her struggle for independence, including William G. Brown, *The Lower South in American History* (New York, 1902); Julian A. C. Chandler *et al*, *The South in the Building of the Nation* (13 vols.; Richmond, 1909–13), Vol. IV; William B. Hesseltine, *The South in American History* (rev. ed.; New York, 1943); and Francis B. Simkins, *A History of the South* (New York, 1953).

A significant body of literature is devoted to an exposition of the weaknesses of the Confederacy. Conflicting political loyalties of the Southern people and leaders are analyzed in Frank Owsley, *State Rights in the Confederacy* (Chicago, 1925). For a study of the Montgomery Convention and the election of Davis and Stephens as Provisional President and Vice President see Albert N. Fitts, "The Confederate Convention" and "The Confederate Convention: The Constitutional Debate," *Alabama Review*, II (April and July, 1949), 83–101, 189–210. Burton J. Hendrick, *Statesmen of the Lost Cause* (New York, 1939), gives vivid sketches of Southern civil leaders along with a telling criticism of their administration. Scholarly and refreshingly sympathetic is Rembert Patrick, *Jefferson Davis and His Cabinet* (Baton Rouge, 1944). Difficulties of raising and maintaining the Southern armies are treated in Albert

Suggested Readings

B. Moore, *Conscription and Conflict in the Confederacy* (New York, 1924). Georgia L. Tatum airs the problem of defection in *Disloyalty in the Confederacy* (Chapel Hill, 1934); and Ella Lonn in *Desertion during the Civil War* (New York, 1928). Analysis of the industrial and economic trials of the Confederacy appears in John C. Schwab, *A Financial and Industrial History of the South during the Civil War* (New York, 1901). Richard C. Todd, *Confederate Finance* (Athens, Georgia, 1954), traces the decline and fall of the Southern monetary system. Frank Vandiver, *Rebel Brass* (Baton Rouge, 1956), tells of Southern efforts to create a successful high command. The same author's *Ploughshares into Swords* (Austin, Tex., 1952) reviews the striking achievements of the Confederate Ordnance Department. Kathleen Bruce, *Virginia Iron Manufacture in the Slave Era* (New York, 1931), gives the story of the Tredegar Works at war. Robert C. Black, III, *Railroads of the Confederacy* (Chapel Hill, 1952), describes the inadequacies of Southern railways and the unsuccessful attempts of the Confederate government to co-ordinate transportation. Flaws in Southern society that impaired her ability to make war are discussed in Charles H. Wesley, *The Collapse of the Confederacy* (Washington, 1937). Bell I. Wiley, *The Road to Appomattox* (Memphis, 1956), exposes mistakes that inclined the Confederacy to defeat.

The most extensive study of Confederate foreign affairs, and the one upon which I have most frequently drawn, is Frank Owsley, *King Cotton Diplomacy* (rev. ed.; Chicago, 1959). A valuable pioneer book on this subject is J. M. Callahan, *The Diplomatic History of the Southern Confederacy* (Baltimore, 1901). Sections on Confederate diplomacy are found in E. D. Adams, *Great Britain and the American Civil War* (2 vols.; London, 1925); and Donaldson Jordan and Edwin J. Pratt, *Europe and the American Civil War* (Boston, 1931).

Vicissitudes of life in the Confederacy are discussed in a number of scholarly volumes. Bell I. Wiley, *The Plain People of the Confederacy* (Baton Rouge, 1944), reveals the trials of life among Southern soldiers and among the home folk, both white and black. Professor Wiley's *Southern Negroes, 1861–1865* (New York, 1938) is an exhaustive and critical treatise on the experience of the Negroes during the war. The same author's *The Life of Johnny Reb* (Indianapolis and New York, 1943) shows the triumphs and

The Confederacy

tribulations of men in the Southern army and gives many insights into the emotions of the people who remained at home. An exposition of the difficulties in Southern industry, finance, and life is in Charles W. Ramsdell, *Behind the Lines in the Southern Confederacy* (Baton Rouge, 1944). Mary E. Massey, *Ersatz in the Confederacy* (Columbia, 1952), gives an interesting account of shortages and substitutes in the blockaded South. The story of Southern women during the war is found in Francis B. Simkins and James W. Patton, *The Women of the Confederacy* (Richmond, 1936); and Katharine M. Jones (ed.), *Heroines of Dixie* (Indianapolis, 1955). Richard B. Harwell (ed.), *Songs of the Confederacy* (New York, 1951), presents the history of Southern war music. The narrative of life and death in the embattled Confederate capital is in Alfred H. Bill, *The Beleaguered City: Richmond, 1861–1865* (New York, 1946). James W. Silver, *Confederate Morale and Church Propaganda* (Tuscaloosa, Ala., 1957), analyzes the role of the churches in leading the South to war and in sustaining the Confederate effort.

Biographies of Confederate civil leaders are rich in the history of the short-lived republic. A definitive biography of Jefferson Davis is yet to be written, but many studies on the Southern President are useful, including William E. Dodd, *Jefferson Davis* (New York, 1907); Hamilton J. Eckenrode, *Jefferson Davis, President of the South* (New York, 1923); Dunbar Rowland (ed.), *Jefferson Davis, Constitutionalist: His Letters, Papers and Speeches* (10 vols.; Jackson, Miss., 1923); Robert W. Winston, *High Stakes and Hair Trigger: The Life of Jefferson Davis* (New York, 1930); Robert McElroy, *Jefferson Davis, the Real and the Unreal* (2 vols.; New York, 1937); and Hudson Strode, *Jefferson Davis* (2 vols.; New York, 1955–59). Accounts of the career of Alexander Stephens are Louis Pendleton, *Alexander H. Stephens* (Philadelphia, 1908); and a skilful Freudian interpretation, Rudolph von Abele, *Alexander H. Stephens: A Biography* (New York, 1946). Other important biographies of Southern figures are Robert D. Meade, *Judah P. Benjamin, Confederate Statesman* (New York, 1943); Laura A. White, *Robert Barnwell Rhett: Father of Secession* (New York, 1931); Percy S. Flippen, *Hershel V. Johnson* (Richmond, 1931); Ulrich B. Phillips, *The Life of Robert Toombs* (New York, 1913); John W. DuBose, *The Life and Times of William Lowndes Yancey*

Suggested Readings

(Birmingham, 1892); and Joseph T. Durkin, *Stephen R. Mallory: Confederate Navy Chief* (Chapel Hill, 1954).

Virtually every Confederate military leader has been the subject of one or more biographies. Greatest of all is Douglas S. Freeman, *R. E. Lee* (4 vols.; New York, 1942–44). The best works on Jackson are George F. R. Henderson, *Stonewall Jackson and the American Civil War* (new ed., 2 vols.; London and New York, 1936); and Frank Vandiver, *Mighty Stonewall* (New York, 1957). Among other interesting and informative biographies are T. H. Williams, *Beauregard, Napoleon in Gray* (Baton Rouge, 1955); John P. Dyer, *"Fightin' Joe" Wheeler* (Baton Rouge, 1941) and *The Gallant Hood* (Indianapolis, 1950); Gilbert Govan and J. W. Livingood, *A Different Valor: The Story of General Joseph E. Johnston* (Indianapolis and New York, 1956); Joseph H. Parks, *General Edmund Kirby Smith* (Baton Rouge, 1954); and Donald B. Sanger and Thomas R. Hay, *James Longstreet* (Baton Rouge, 1952).

Histories of individual Southern states during the Civil War provide much information on the Confederacy. Among the most rewarding of these are Walter L. Fleming, *Civil War and Reconstruction in Alabama* (Cleveland, 1911); William W. Davis, *The Civil War and Reconstruction in Florida* (New York, 1913); E. Merton Coulter, *The Civil War and Readjustment in Kentucky* (Chapel Hill, 1926); David Y. Thomas, *Arkansas in War and Reconstruction* (Little Rock, Ark., 1926); James W. Patton, *Unionism and Reconstruction in Tennessee, 1860–1869* (Chapel Hill, 1934); Jefferson Davis Bragg, *Louisiana in the Confederacy* (Baton Rouge, 1941); John K. Bettersworth, *Confederate Mississippi* (Baton Rouge, 1943); and Charles E. Cauthen, *South Carolina Goes to War, 1860–1865* (Chapel Hill, 1950).

Acknowledgments

I am indebted to Professor Bell Irvin Wiley of Emory University, who once taught me Civil War history and introduced me to research in the subject, for reading the manuscript of this book and suggesting ways to improve it. I am grateful to Professor Hugh F. Rankin of Tulane University for encouraging me to write the book and for offering sound advice on portions of the manuscript. I appreciate the efforts of my wife, Allie Lee Roland, who has been a sympathetic and candid reader of the manuscript. I wish to thank Professor Daniel J. Boorstin of the University of Chicago, editor of the series in which the book appears, for his helpful comments on the manuscript.

Index

Index

Army of Tennessee: withdraws to Georgia, 134; destroyed, 178; mentioned, 183, 186
Army of the Potomac, 138
Arsenals, Confederate, 69, 135
Atlanta, Georgia: threatened by Sherman, 139; defended by Joseph E. Johnston, 140; lost by Confederates, 147; mentioned, 146, 171–73, *passim*, 183
Augusta, Georgia: Davis speaks in, 173

Banks, Nathaniel P.: attacks in Louisiana, 138; Red River campaign defeated, 140; opinion of Southern women, 167
Baptist church: divided over slavery, 8; mentioned, 159
Barksdale, Ethelbert: supports Davis, 62; offers bill to suspend writ of habeas corpus, 77; supports use of Negro troops, 184
Barnard, Frederick A. P., 162
Barnwell, Robert: supports Davis, 62
"Battle of Charleston Harbor, The" (poem), 155
Beauregard, P. G. T.: takes Fort Sumter, 30; advocates offensive warfare, 39; achieves distinction in Confederacy, 39; offended by Benjamin, 64; description of, 95; opinion of Commissary General Northrop, 97; heroic stand at Petersburg, 139; attacks Benjamin F. Butler, 140
Belgium, 104
Bell, John, 11, 14, 86
Benét, Stephen Vincent: describes John Bell Hood, 146
Benjamin, Judah P.: Confederate Attorney General, 28; attacked by Congress, 61; Confederate Secretary of War, 61; offends generals, 64; Confederate Secretary of State, 64; opinion of Joseph E. Johnston, 83; seeks diplomatic recognition of Confederacy, 111, 112; seeks French support, 113; withdraws emissary from England, 122; mentioned, 114, 118, 120, 123, 136, 182, 183, 185, 187
Beresford-Hope, Alexander James Beresford, 107
Bermuda Hundred, 140
Bill of Rights, 26
Bingham, William: publishes Latin grammar, 162
Bingham School, 162
Blair, Francis P., 181
Blockade, Union, 36, 103, 104, 106, 111, 113, 136, 137, 179, 191
Blockade-runners, 136–37
Bocock, Thomas S.: supports Davis, 62
"Bonnie Blue Flag, The," 158
Boyce, William W., 180
Boyd, Belle, 168
Bragg, Braxton: imposes martial law, 77; joins Albert Sidney Johnston, 79; Kentucky campaign, 80–81; battle of Murfreesboro, 84; supported by Davis, 97; description of, 97–98; wins battle of Chickamauga, 125; loses Chattanooga, 125–26; becomes military adviser to Davis, 134
Brazil: produces cotton, 123
Breckinridge, John C.: presidential candidate in 1860, 11; receives Louisiana electoral votes, 14; at battle of New Market, Virginia, 140; Confederate Secretary of War, 187
Bright, John, 108, 111, 119
British consuls: expelled from Confederacy, 122
British government: rejects French armistice proposal, 118. *See also* England; Diplomacy; King Cotton
British Parliament: faction of, supports Confederacy, 107
Brockenburn, 157

Index

Index

Index

Index

Index

Index

Kentucky: refuses to secede, 33; invaded by Bragg, 80–81
Key West, Florida, 29
King Cotton. *See* Diplomacy, King Cotton
Kirby Smith, Edmund: commander of Trans-Mississippi Department, 126–27; surrender of, 190; mentioned, 91, 140, 184
Kirby-Smithdom. *See* Trans-Mississippi Department

Lairds: shipbuilders of Birkenhead, 119
Lane, Joseph, 11
Lawton, Alexander R., 133
Lead: source of, 66
LeConte, John, 161–62
LeConte, Joseph, 161–62
Lee, Robert E.: Winston Churchill's opinion of, 39; urges conscription, 58; at Second Manassas, 63; invades Maryland, 73, 115; offers liberation to Maryland, 80; at Fredericksburg, 83; at Gettysburg, 85; praised by Senate, 133; a hero in spite of defeats, 135; in battle of the Wilderness, 138; a devout Christian, 159; defends Petersburg, 176; made General in Chief, 179; urges use of Negro troops, 184; abandons Petersburg, 189; surrender of, 189; inspiring leadership of, 194; mentioned, 66, 84, 91, 92, 94, 97, 118, 130, 139, 142, 171, 172, 178, 180, 188
Letcher, John, 32
Liberator, The, 7
Lincoln, Abraham: debates with Douglas, 11; elected President of United States, 11; reinforces Fort Sumter, 29; calls for troops, 30; proclaims blockade, 103; frees Mason and Slidell, 106; doubtful of re-election, 141; and Emancipation Proclamation, 166; re-elected President, 173; at Hampton Roads Conference, 181; mentioned, 2, 12, 31, 32, 57, 73, 76, 86, 93, 108, 118, 134, 144, 146, 180, 182, 191, 192
Lindsay, William S., 107, 112, 121
Literature, Confederate, 154–57
"Little Giffen," 155
London: Hotze arrives in, 109; mentioned, 185
Longstreet, James, 179
Lookout Mountain: battle of, 125, 126
"Lorena," 158
Louisiana: secession of, 15; Creoles of, 95, 105; Federal occupation of, 126; Banks's offensive in, 138; Red River campaign, 140; mentioned, 3, 9, 10, 14
Louisiana State Seminary and Military Academy, 162
Louisville, Kentucky, 80
Lovell, Mansfield, 76
Lutheran church, 159

Macaria; or, Altars of Sacrifice, 156
McCarthy, Harry, 158
McClellan, George B.: repulsed at Richmond, 63, 74; in the east, 66; at Sharpsburg, 80; presidential candidate, 140; mentioned, 180
McCord, Louisa Susanna, 169
McGuire, Judith White, 157
Macon, Georgia, 173
Macon, Nathaniel, 5
Magnolia Cemetery, Charleston: mentioned, 155
Malaria, 152
Mallet, John W., 161
Mallory, Stephen R.: Confederate Secretary of Navy, 27, 64, 119
Manassas: first battle of, 49, 56, 95, 149; second battle of, 63, 74, 96, 115
Manchester Guardian, 108
Manifesto: by Southern congressmen, 4

Index

Mann, A. Dudley, 102, 104
Manufacturing. *See* Industry, Southern
Manufacturing and Direct Trade Association of the Confederate States, 69
Martial law, 76, 77
Martinsburg, Virginia, 168
Maryland: remains in Union, 33; invasion of, by Lee, 73, 80, 115
"Maryland, My Maryland," 156, 158
Mason, George, 105
Mason, James M.: Confederate emissary, 105; captured, 106; arrives in England, 107; fails to gain recognition of confederacy, 115; advised to transfer iron-clads, 120; leaves England, 122; interview with Palmerston, 186; mentioned, 109, 110, 121, 185
Matamoros, Mexico, 105
Maximilian: Emperor of Mexico, 105, 123
Meade, George Gordon, 85
Medical supplies, 136, 152
Memminger, Christopher G.: Confederate Secretary of the Treasury, 27; financial problems of, 44–48, 71–72, 131–32; resignation of, 174; mentioned, 18, 64, 88, 89
Mercier, Count Henri, 109, 112, 116
Mercury (Charleston): advocates offensive warfare, 52; attacks Davis, 75; supports conscription, 86; criticizes method of taxation, 131; opposes administration, 145; Robert Barnwell Rhett, Jr., editor of, 145; charges Davis with incompetence, 157; urges Lee be made chief executive, 179; denounces use of Negro troops, 184–85; mentioned, 2, 3, 12, 53, 78, 82, 88
Methodist church, 8, 159
Methodist Episcopal Church, South, 8
Mexican War, 7, 22

Mexico, 7, 8, 104, 105, 109, 114, 123, 127, 181
Military leadership: South rich in, 39
Military supplies, 136. *See also* Blockade-runners; Industry, Southern
Milton, John: Governor of Florida, 59, 142
Missionary Ridge: battle of, 125–26
Mississippi: secession of, 13; unprotected, 127; mentioned, 3, 4
Mississippi River: exposes South to invasion, 37; controlled by Federals, 126; mentioned, 127
Mississippi Valley: defense of, by Albert Sidney Johnston, 78; mentioned, 84
Missouri: remains in Union, 33; mentioned, 54
Missouri Compromise, 7, 32
Mitchell, Margaret, 148, 156
Mobile, Alabama, 79
Money: measures for raising, 149. *See also* Confederate finance
Monroe Doctrine, 181
Montgomery, Alabama, 16, 17
Montgomery Convention: activities of, 16–27
Moore, M. B., 162
Morale: of the South, 41, 90, 140, 148, 149, 157; of the North, 140–41
Moscow, 173
Mother's Parting Words to Her Soldier Boy, A (religious tract), 160–61
Munitions, 36, 68. *See also* Industry, Southern; Arms
Murfreesboro: battle of, 98
Music, 158
Myers, Abraham C., 133

Napoleon III: covets Mexico, 109; interviews with Slidell, 110, 121; considers intervention, 112; of-

Index

Index

scription, 58; condemns Congress, 75; mentioned, 82, 134, 182
Population: Northern and Southern compared, 34
Potomac River, 84
Prairie Grove: battle of, 84
Prayer: encouraged by Confederate government, 160
Presbyterian church, 159
Presidential election of 1864, 140, 173–74
Preston, John S., 144
Preston, William, 123
Prisoners, 126
Produce Loan, 47, 71
Propaganda, Confederate. See Confederate propaganda
Propagandist, British, 108
Propagandist, Confederate, 108
Provisional Congress, 18, 27, 58
Provisional Constitution, 18
Provisional Government, 18, 49, 53
Provisional President, 19
Provisional Vice President, 19

Quartermaster Department, 167
Quartermaster General, 133
Queen Victoria, 103

Railroads: South's inadequacies, 37; maintenance, 138
Raleigh, North Carolina, 142
Randall, James Ryder, 156
Randolph, George Wythe: Confederate Secretary of War, 65; supports conscription, 79, 80; resigns, 81; views on strategy, 82
Randolph, John, 5
Rapidan River, 138, 140
Reagan, John H.: Confederate Postmaster General, 28, 64
Red River campaign, 140
Refugees, 151
Register (Mobile), 108
Relief, 153
Religion, 158–61, 164
Religious tracts, 160–61
Republican party, 11

Resaca: battle of, 139–40
Rhett, Robert Barnwell: "fireeater," 10; calls convention, 16; helps draft constitution, 25; on secession, 27; criticizes administration, 49, 53, 55; advocates conscription, 58; retires, 145; mentioned, 8, 12, 17, 19, 20, 51, 52, 56, 63, 82, 134, 184
Rhett, Robert Barnwell, Jr., 145
Rhodes, James Ford, 191
Richmond, Virginia: capital of Confederacy, 48; falls to Federals, 188–89; mentioned, 50, 53, 67, 76, 83, 116, 135, 140, 142, 164, 165, 178, 187
Roanoke Island, 54, 111
Roebuck, John A., 107, 121, 122
Roman, André, 28
Rosecrans, William: at Corinth, 80; at Murfreesboro, 84; at Chickamauga, 125
Rost, Pierre, 102, 104
Russell, John, 103, 111, 112, 115–17, *passim*, 120, 122
Russell, William Howard, 41, 101
Ryan, Abram J., 155

St. Elmo, 156
St. Paul's Episcopal Church, 188
Santo Domingo, 166
Savannah, Georgia, 177
Schofield, John M., 177–78
Schools, 162–63
Scott, Sir Walter, 158
Sculpture, Confederate, 158
Secession, 3, 4, 27
Sectionalism, 7
Seddon, James Alexander: Confederate Secretary of War, 82; ideas on strategy, 83–84; mentioned, 94, 183, 184
Selma, Alabama, 135
Sentinel (Richmond), 157
Seven Pines: battle of, 94
Seward, William H., 29, 112, 114, 116, 117, 123, 181
Shakespeare, William, 158

Index